The Micheli...
An Unauthorized Advertisi...

Rudy LeCoadic

Dedication

To my wife Melanie, whose enthusiasm for life is legendary, and our sons, Félix, five years old, who thinks people that don't collect anything are weird, and Lucas, two-and-a-half years old, who believes that Bibendum is a member of the family.

Copyright © 2005 by Rudy LeCoadic
Library of Congress Control Number: 2005927640

    All rights reserved. No part of this work may be reproduced or used in any form or by any means—graphic, electronic, or mechanical, including photocopying or information storage and retrieval systems—without written permission from the publisher.
    The scanning, uploading and distribution of this book or any part thereof via the Internet or via any other means without the permission of the publisher is illegal and punishable by law. Please purchase only authorized editions and do not participate in or encourage the electronic piracy of copyrighted materials.
    "Schiffer," "Schiffer Publishing Ltd. & Design," and the "Design of pen and ink well" are registered trademarks of Schiffer Publishing Ltd.

Covers and book designed by Bruce Waters
Type set in Benguiat Gothic heading font/text font Korinna.

ISBN: 0-7643-2299-0
Printed in China

    "The Michelin® Man, Bibendum" is a registered trademark of the Michelin® Company.
    The text and products pictured in this book are from the collection of the author of this book and various private collectors. This book is not sponsored, endorsed or otherwise affiliated with "The Michelin® Company" or any of the companies whose products are represented herein.

Published by Schiffer Publishing Ltd.
4880 Lower Valley Road
Atglen, PA 19310
Phone: (610) 593-1777; Fax: (610) 593-2002
E-mail: Info@schifferbooks.com

For the largest selection of fine reference books on this and related subjects, please visit our web site at
www.schifferbooks.com
We are always looking for people to write books on new and related subjects. If you have an idea for a book please contact us at the above address.

This book may be purchased from the publisher.
Include $3.95 for shipping.
Please try your bookstore first.
You may write for a free catalog.

In Europe, Schiffer books are distributed by
Bushwood Books
6 Marksbury Ave.
Kew Gardens
Surrey TW9 4JF England
Phone: 44 (0) 20 8392-8585; Fax: 44 (0) 20 8392-9876
E-mail: info@bushwoodbooks.co.uk
Free postage in the U.K., Europe; air mail at cost.

Contents

Introduction — 5

My Start — 6

Rarity versus Condition — 7

Foreign or American? — 8

Grading the Condition — 9

Using the Rarity Guide — 9

Using the Price Guide — 9

Chapter One: Paper Posters and Cardboard Signs — 10

Chapter Two: Porcelain, Tin, and Wooden Signs — 21

Chapter Three: Tins, Containers, and Tools — 48

Chapter Four: Clocks and Calendars — 72

Chapter Five: Smalls — 77

Chapter Six: Figural Displays — 96

Chapter Seven: Paper Items — 116

Chapter Eight: The Ultimate Tribute — 168

Chapter Nine: The Archives — 171

Final Words — 175

Bibliography — 176

Index — 176

The Contributors

I am very fortunate that some of you allowed me to photograph the rarest pieces from your collections, while others took it upon themselves to provide me with great images. I am also honored that such a great international group of passionate collectors have allowed me to share their knowledge and collections with others through this book. I thank you my friends.

The Bibendum Restaurant Limited, England. For providing great images to showcase the Bibendum House on such short notice.

Pau Medrano Bigas, Spain. For providing great photographs, information, and stories, and for showing so much enthusiasm for this project.

Luc Buisson and Olivier Lapous of "La Joubantique," France. For allowing me to photograph some of your items.

Martin Burger, Australia. For sharing your extensive collection and giving me your support from the very beginning.

Dean Schmide. For photographing the Martin Burger collection

Damian James Cessario, Australia. For your knowledge of the mascots, for providing photos of some unique pieces in your collection, and for your much-appreciated support.

Damien Delabre of Around the World Antiques, France. For bringing some of your collection to the states just so that I could photograph it.

Juan de San Román, Responsible de Patrimonio Histórico de Michelin, para España y Portugal. For providing unique, original images.

Gilles Dutto, France. For allowing me to photograph some very rare items out of your collection and sharing a passion.

Emmanuel Lopez of Gallery Estampe Moderne et Sportive, France. For allowing me to photograph your very rare poster.

Pascal Eveno, France. For providing me with many items over the years and allowing me to photograph your sign.

Robert J Harrington, USA. For allowing me to photograph some amazingly rare items out of your extensive automobilia collection.

Brian E. Harto, USA. For allowing me to photograph your collection and sharing your knowledge on the history of Michelin in Milltown.

Etienne Levillain, France. For allowing me to photograph some very scarce items from your collection.

Giovanni Longo, France. For your help in photographing your collection.

The Milltown Museum and Historical Society, USA. For allowing me to photograph some of your collection.

David Ralph, England. For providing me with photos of your extensive collection.

Tomonari Sakurai of Grays, France. For providing me with photos of rare items and sharing many stories over the years.

Peggy and Ed Strauss, USA. For allowing me to photograph your impressive collection and your enthusiasm for this project.

Tony Wraight of Finesse Fine Art, England. For providing me with high quality images of a very unique mascot.

Special thanks to my friends Jacob Dresner and George Hertz of Adorama Rental Department in New York City, for their long time support and help in this project. They were the photography equipment rental and supplies source for the making of this book.

Special thanks to my friends at "CRC" the Color Resource Center in New York City for their long time support. The majority of the film processing was handled by CRC.

Introduction

Most people are surprised when they learn that the Michelin company was founded in France in 1832. Bibendum came in a bit later, in 1898, when Édouard and André Michelin found their inspiration in a stack of tires ranging in sizes, neatly displayed during an exposition. The form of a man was evident, only lacking arms and legs.

They hired the services of an artist named Marius Rossillon (1867-1947), who at that time was creating advertising images under the pseudonym O'Galop. He adapted one of his creations believed to have been originally for a brewery, hence the famous phrase "Nunc est Bibendum" which translates from Latin as "now it's time to drink". The round-shaped man, made of tires raising a glass full of nails and glass shards was flanked on either side by characters designed similarly but much smaller and sickly, likely to have represented his concurrence. The phrase "Le pneu Michelin boit l'obstacle" was added below, which literally translated means "The Michelin tire drinks the obstacle".

The Michelin man, soon known as Bibendum, was born. His first introduction was in a black and white newspaper ad, where he was shown driving a car. The next was in the form of the poster that was designed by O'Galop, and used for years, occasionally adding accessories like tins of rubber cement, tools, and a compressed air bottle to the foreground, until 1914 when the last version was printed with a blue background. But this was not the last of O'Galop, As you are about to discover we owe him credit for many of our most prized collectibles, as he became the principal graphic artist for the Michelin brothers. One thing was for certain Michelin had found in Bibendum the perfect spokesman and was about to reward him with immortality. Bibendum was voted by an international panel in the 1990s most recognizable and oldest advertising character in the world, having been in continuous use since his creation in 1898.

My Start

The collection started in the mid to late 1980s with a series of impulse buys. I had no real intentions, at first, of starting a new collection. I was already collecting various soda brands signs, advertising figures and toys; the Bibendum just reminded me of my native land. The first Bibendum piece I ever came across was a Bakelite ashtray with Bib seated at the back. Next came a truck figure from the 40s found at Brimfield, and a few months later, at a Pennsylvania toy show, I bought a great 1940s tin sign with Bib riding a motorcycle from a Spanish dealer. I went home that day and put all three pieces together and that really did it; I wanted more… lots more!

I called every advertising dealer I knew in the U.S., asking if they had anything Michelin, but no one had anything to offer. I realized that they had never sold anything memorable or at least worth mentioning.

With the fast growing interest of gas and oil collectibles, shows became more frequent and specialized auctions started to emerge. I was finally able to network with people that at least had interest and knowledge of some advertising pieces in collections. I met a few French dealers that had started coming into the United States on a regular basis, setting up at Hershey and Brimfield. They specialized in early automobilia and, much to my delight, they always had Michelin items for sale.

My real beginner's luck story happened in Paris. I bought a newspaper on antiques, and found an advertisement for a 1930s Michelin die-cut cardboard sign. In this window or counter display, Bib was dressed as a child in a sailor's outfit. The price was $400 and the seller lived a train ride away, so off I went. When I got there the cardboard sign was on the kitchen table looking fantastic! Of course I bought it, and when I asked the man if he knew much about Michelin or where I could find other things for sale, every collector's dream come true. He led me to a room and pushed the door open.

"Voila!" To my amazement I found myself in a room filled with Michelin signs, tins, ashtrays and figures, the whole works! It was much more than I had ever imagined finding in one place. WOW! I asked if he would sell anything and he answered, "I'll sell all of it!". Next came the fear that he wanted to sell the whole thing for one money, because in the huge amount of items in his collection, laid some real dead ringers and many more recent items, along with piles of magazines. But it wasn't the case. Everything had come up for sale a week before and I was the first one there. I know that for a fact, because of the layer of dust covering everything. The pricing seemed, generally, to be based on size. I bought just about everything old in that room, even things I already had in the collection for fear of having regrets later. Besides the price was right! I think I walked out with more than 50 pre-1950s items, ranging from 3-dimensional figures of Bibs to a 1920s mint double-sided tin sign. He was happy with his money, but I was happier!

that had some problems, hoping to upgrade later. Twelve years have passed, and they're still on my wall. If I hadn't bought I would be kicking myself for passing on them, because I have never had the opportunity to buy others like them. The rarity scale in the book is a very important tool, hopefully keeping you from walking away from a sign that you may never see again because of a chip or rust spot.

Rarity Versus Condition

Collecting Bibendum differs in many aspects from collecting other advertising memorabilia, so you may find yourself relearning or changing your mind about some points that you felt very strongly about. Condition of a sign was key for me as I know it is for most advertising collectors. Anything under the grade of 8 or excellent was unacceptable, because, let's face it, even a rare soda sign turns up a few times a year.

While the condition of a Michelin piece still drastically affects the value, it should be a minimal factor when assessing desirability in the case of a rare item, i.e. a sign in condition 7 is still very acceptable; though you should be able to pick it up for a reasonable price. You can always change your mind later, sell it, or you may be lucky enough one day to get a chance to upgrade. It beats the alternative of just passing it up, maybe missing the opportunity to have it in your collection. We don't have the luxury that we had with soda signs to wait for the perfect example in mint condition. Waiting around for mint signs may lead to regret and frustration. A few years ago I bought with much hesitation some early signs

Foreign or American?

The majority of Michelin advertising pieces between 1900s and 1960s are French in origin, but not all. Many were made in the countries where they were meant to be distributed or displayed. Many giveaways and signs were made in the US and are, of course, my favorites, but don't shy away from European items; you would be robbing yourself of the finest advertising signs and memorabilia related to automobiles. It may take some time getting used to, but collecting Michelin isn't about collecting Americana, Bibendum from the very start was an international celebrity. Michelin opened factories and headquarters throughout the world at an amazing speed, including France in 1832, England in 1904, Turin, Italy in 1906, and Milltown, New Jersey in the USA in 1907. Many signs, posters, and giveaways in foreign languages or with no text at all, were also produced in France to be exported as advertising for their products elsewhere in the world. Tire pressure gauges and puncture repair kits also came with directions in several languages.

Most Michelin items are of superior quality, and designed specifically for the company rather than some as generic giveaway with the Bibendum stamped on it. In the early years owning a car wasn't within everyone's reach and, therefore, the advertising had to appeal to an elite clientele. All over the world Michelin not only produced advertising signs but a long line of advertising giveaways and merchandise, including toys for children in the effigy of the Bibendum. While you will rarely find an item from the Michelin Company without Bib on it, you will find him without the Michelin name.

American advertising is found from 1907 through the early 1930s, and then there is nothing until the 1960s. This is because the Milltown New Jersey factory closed in 1930, during the Depression.

Grading the Condition

Trying to communicate the condition of an item can get very confusing without a good photo. In the case of an auction catalog the image is usually so small that scratches and marks don't even show. This often leads to confusion, misunderstanding and most often a waste of time for everyone. Since condition is so important when evaluating whether or not you are willing to pay the price for something, it is important to be accurate. When dealing with a foreign collector or dealer, I found it best to use a scale 5 thru 10, 10 being best condition possible and 5 being worst condition, it is a system that seems to be universal and most of all it is relevant to a wide range of collectors. The basic chart below should be helpful:

10	Mint	Perfect, no marks, no flaws or sign of age whatsoever
9	Near Mint	Near perfect, very minor hardly noticeable marks
8	Excellent	Nice condition, small scratches or chips or minor fading
7	Very good	Noticeable problems, bends, rust or stains, still acceptable
6	Good	Evident damage and aging, creases, folds, holes, etc…
5	Poor	Very severe damage, usually no value

Both of these systems are often used more precisely. For example, 8.5 would have an equivalent of Excellent +.

10	Only one example known to me
9	Very rare, less than 10 known to me
8	Rare
7	Hard to find
6	Obtainable
5	Common
4	Very common

Using the Price Guide

When a price guide is written for an international group of collectors, many factors affect it, including geography, economy and trends. I have based this price guide on an item in excellent or 8.0 condition (see condition guide). Therefore, one in lesser condition would be worth considerably less and one in better condition would be worth considerably more. The US$ amount after the description of an item is not for the item photographed but for what someone could expect to pay for one like it in excellent condition at auction or from a dealer. Rarity also plays a role in determining a value; if, in the future, an item is found in large quantities it is no longer as rare and, therefore, is worth considerably less. I tried to be as accurate and consistent as possible. It was by far the most difficult part of this book, and I hope you will find it comprehensive and useful. It is however only a guide and the author accepts no responsibility for any gain or loss the reader may experience as a result of using this guide.

Using the Rarity Guide

At the end of the description of each item, you will find a "Rarity" rating, based on how many pieces in excellent or better condition I have encountered or have knowledge of in collections, both in the United States and abroad. I believe this important information will be very useful. It seems to be accurate although it is based on my personal experience and new finds are made everyday. It is however only a guide and the author accepts no responsibility for any gain or loss the reader may experience as a result of using this guide.

Chapter One
Paper Posters and Cardboard Signs

From the birth of Bibendum in 1898 until 1914 this poster by O'Galop was produced in different sizes, with many variants. Some later examples with blue backgrounds show some of the accessories available at that time, such as rubber cement, tools, compressed air bottles, and pressure gauges. Earlier examples like this one simply demonstrate how the Michelin man is able to drink the obstacles unlike his competitors who are portrayed here as sickly and weak. The example shown was meant to be displayed indoors. It originally came coated with a thin layer of varnish and had a thin metal hanger on the top and bottom. Unfortunately this was usually trimmed off by poster dealers to facilitate the mounting on linen. The usual size is 47" x 63". The poster shown here measures 14" x 17" without the metal hangers and was offered in 1907, printed by Imp. Lemercier, Paris. All these different versions are equally rare, however the earliest versions are the most sought after making them the most expensive, this is also how the Michelin man became known as Bibendum.

1907 paper hanger poster by O'Galop. Rarity 9. $1,500; with original hangers add. $250. Larger 1898 to 1914 paper posters by O'Galop. Rarity 8-9. $2,500 to $4,000

1905 paper poster by O'Galop, known as "Le coup de Semelle." Usually seen in a much larger format of 47" x 63" with either a red or blue background, this version is only 23" x 31" with a burgundy background. Also notice the absence of text, suggesting that this poster was to be displayed overseas. *Courtesy "Gallery Estampe Moderne et Sportive."*. Rarity 10

Paper poster by O'Galop, Imp Chaix, Paris, 1911. Several slight variations of this poster exist, differing mostly in the shading of the background and without the O'Galop signature. Either way it is a favorite classic image. France 32" x 47 1/2". Rarity 8. $1,250

Cardboard display, c. 1910. Very scarce cardboard stringer for displaying tire repair tins. One of the earliest advertising pieces, showing not one but six Bibendums. France, 14 3/4" x 10 1/2". *Collection Damien Delabre*. Rarity 10.

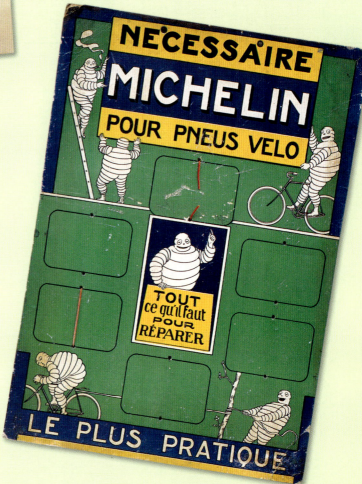

Paper poster, 1911. Anonymous artist, Imp. Chaix, Paris. This poster is rarely seen, possibly because it was designed as an indoor poster. The quality and durability of the paper may have been less than its outdoor counterparts. France, 23 1/2" x 30 1/2". *Collection Damien Delabre.* Rarity 9. $1,250

Paper poster by Roowy, Imp Chaix, Paris, 1912. One of the most appealing posters for its unusual 3-D effect. France, 31" x 47". Rarity 8. $1,250

Paper poster, anonymous artist, printed by Modiano, Milano, 1919. By far my favorite poster. Even though the artwork was inspired by Roowie's earlier poster, the beauty and quality seen here surpasses it. This is one you wouldn't get tired of looking at. Italy, 27 1/2" x 39". Rarity 10. $2,500

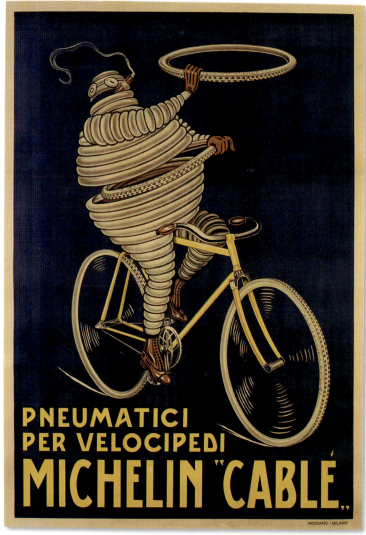

Paper poster by F. Fabiano, Imp. Chaix, Paris, 1916. One of very few posters showing a woman. France, 31 1/2" x 47 1/2". Rarity 7. $1,000

Paper poster, anonymous artist, 1923. This unusual sepia poster is rarely seen in excellent condition. France, 27 1/2" x 20 3/4". Rarity 8. $550

Paper poster, anonymous artist, 1926. Note the lack of text, a sure sign that this poster would have been destined for export to display in many different countries. France, 31 1/2" x 45 1/2". Rarity 9. $2,500

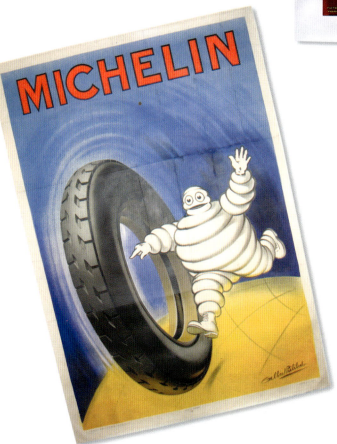

Paper poster by Albert Philibert, Imp. L. Serre & Cie, Paris, 1925. This very scarce poster was the introduction of the familiar image of Bibendum running along side of a tire, a design used for decades as the Michelin logo. France, 70" x 49". Rarity 9. $2,500

Cardboard stringer, Imp. Henon, 1927. A very scarce piece with great colors and industrial graphics. Very large vertical and horizontal paper posters, both in French and English with the same artwork were also produced. France. Cardboard hanger: 19 3/4" x 29 3/4". Rarity 10. $750. Poster versions: Rarity 8. $1,000

Cardboard stringer, 1927. This one is a mystery so far as what it may have held, but it was most likely tire inflation charts. France, 15 3/4" x 23 1/2". *Collection "La Joubantique."* Rarity 10. $125

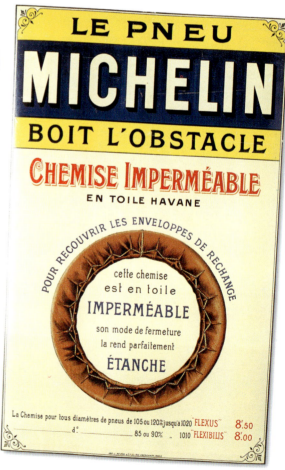

Paper hanger, c. 1910. Imp. L. Revon. France, 18 1/4" x 11 1/4". *Collection Damien Delabre.* Rarity 9

Paper poster, 1923. Michelin tourism offices offered itineraries showing best routes, sceneries, hotels, and restaurants to assist drivers in their journeys. France, 20 1/2" x 28". Collection "La Joubantique". Rarity 8. $550

Cardboard die-cut with easel back, Imp. H Bouquet, Paris, 1920s. Scarce sign designed for window displays and car showrooms; the sign was available in 3 different sizes. France, 47" x 36". Rarity 10

Rare cardboard die-cut, Imp. Bouquet, Paris, 1920s. Not much here was left out, advertising maps and guides, the Michelin wheel, Cablé tires, and tubes. A great graphic piece with vibrant colors. France, 33 1/2" x 27 1/2". Rarity 9. $900

Paper poster, Imp. Serre & Cie, 1928. A reminder to inflate your tires the 1st and 15th of the month; a great poster to display with your compressor. France, 22 1/2" x 15". Rarity 7. $300

Cardboard die-cut, rubber ball counter display, Imp. H. Bouquet, Paris, 1932. The back has an illustration showing how the display was to be set up. France, 24" x 15 1/2". Rarity 9. $650

Cardboard sign advertising rubber balls, 1932. France, 16" x 24". Rarity 9. $125

Round cardboard sign, 1932, designed to fit inside a bicycle tire for display. 26 3/4" diameter, France. *Collection "La Joubantique."* Rarity 10. $200

Thin cardboard poster by F. Fetti, Milan, 1951. An unusually late image for Bib to be smoking a cigar. Italy, 27 1/2" x 39 1/2". Rarity 9. $700

Paper poster for motorcycle tires, 1955. Anonymous, Imp. Kapp, France. 30 3/4" x 15 1/8". Rarity 9. $300

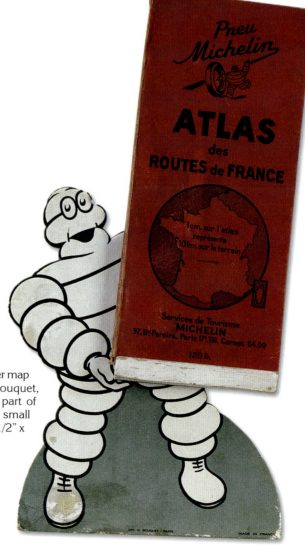

Cardboard stand-up counter map display, 1960, Imp. H. Bouquet, Paris. Note the map isn't part of the display, it rests on a small wooden ledge. France 14 1/2" x 5 1/2". Rarity 8. $100

Chapter Two
Porcelain, Tin and Wooden Signs

Very scarce double-sided embossed tin sign, Imp. L. Revon, Paris, c. 1910. It is shown here with its hanger sign. No doubt one of the best Michelin sign, only a handful are known to have survived. On this version the words "pneus and velo" are not embossed. France, 26 3/4" x 18 3/4". Rarity 9. $1,500

Double-sided embossed tin sign, Imp. Alfred Riom & Cie, Nantes, c. 1910. This version of this very scarce sign is fully embossed. France, 26" x 19". *Collection Gilles Dutto.* Rarity 9. $1,500

Fully embossed tin sign, Metalgraph GR, Milano, 1919. Where to begin? With amazing graphics, the quality of the litho and the finesse of the details are stunning. Clearly, in my opinion, this is the best Michelin sign. I owned the paper poster with the same graphic, never expecting that one day an unknown tin version would surface. Italy, 19.5" x 13.5". Rarity 10

Double-sided tin sign, Louis Cannard, c. 1915. One of the earliest and best designed signs, it is rarely found in any condition. I purchased this one relentlessly below grade when I first started collecting, hoping to be able to upgrade soon after, but that never happened. Looking back it was a good purchase. France, 19" x 27". Rarity 9. $900

Tin sign, manufactured by De Andreis, c. 1919. I had never seen or heard of this sign prior to taking this photo for the book. France, 27 1/2" x 21 1/4". *Collection Etienne Levillain.* Rarity 10

Double-sided tin sign, Louis Cannard, c. 1920. This sign was most likely used to announce the price of gas that day. A version of this sign in German also exists. France, 19 1/4" x 15 3/4". Rarity 9. $750

Double-sided tin sign, Louis Cannard, 1926. Another gorgeous double-sided sign, also made in a very rare embossed version. France, 29 1/2" x 29 1/2". Version shown: Rarity 8. $900. Embossed version: Rarity 9. $1,200

Double-sided tin die-cut sign, Louis Cannard, 1929. A small sign would have hung from the two holes at the bottom indicating the year the stock was last updated. France, 29 1/2" x 30". Rarity 9. $ 1,000

Very scarce double-sided tin flange sign, 1927, much smaller than its hanging counterpart, it was also manufactured by Louis Cannard but for export. This superb example was found in Australia. France, 25" long. *Collection Damian J Cessario*. Rarity 10

Another very scarce tin double-sided flange sign, this one manufactured by De Andreis, late 1920s. It is identical to the one made by Louis Cannard with the exception that this has complete lack of text other than "Michelin." Eliminating the constraints of the French or English language, this sign made for export and was displayable anywhere in the world. France, 25 1/2" x 22 1/2". Rarity 10

Very impressive embossed die-cut tin sign with easel back, G. de Andreis, late 1920s to early 1930s. This very scarce, completely embossed tin die-cut sign would have stood on sidewalks outside of dealerships and service stations, announcing both prices of tires and gas. It is only when looking at a mint example that you can see the subtlety of the wide range of pale colors, used to give this sign an outstanding 3-D effect. Unfortunately the pale colors would have been the first to fade away in the sun. France, 67" x 38". Rarity 9. $2,500

Double-sided stock tin sign. Chas. W. Shonk Litho, Chicago, c. 1910. It may not have the greatest graphics, but nevertheless it is among the rarest signs. This is the only one I have ever seen, but it is illustrated in many magazine ads hanging on garages. This leads me to believe that it was widely distributed through the 1920s. USA, 28" diameter. Rarity 10. $500

Tin die-cut flange sign, c. 1920. A spectacular sign with a very life-like Bibendum. No doubt the best designed Michelin flange sign. USA, 23" x 21.5". *Collection Robert J Harrington.* Rarity 10.

Porcelain double-sided flange sign, c. 1915. This very sign hung on the Michelin Factory in Milltown, New Jersey until the plant closed in 1930. USA, 23" x 19". *Collection Brian E Harto.* Rarity 10. (Beware of single-sided reproductions)

Porcelain double-sided flange sign, 1920s. With its fantastic Bib smoking his cigar, this is a must for the American collector regardless of condition. USA, 23" x 19". Rarity 9. $1,300

Tin double-sided flange sign, American Art Works, Coshocton, Ohio, 1920s. This tin flange is much rarer than its porcelain counterpart. USA, 26" x 19". Rarity 9. $1,200

Tin-die cut tire holder, 1920s. An unbelievable sign designed to hold a tire in a showroom or window display. Only a handful are known to exist. This much sought after piece is appreciated by a wide range of advertising collectors. USA, 19" x 17 1/2". Rarity 9. $1,500

Heavy wooden, sand-painted sign, Cross Press and Signs, c. 1910. This very early and scarce American sign had tinted sand applied to the wet paint giving it a rough and durable surface. USA, 36" x 12". Rarity 9. $1,200

Embossed tin tacker sign, New York Signs, c. 1927. This type of sign can have a variety of car manufacturer's and dealer's addresses on it, which could greatly affect the value depending of the name of the car it advertises. La Salle is shown here. USA, 11 1/2" x 35 1/2". Rarity 9. $800

Embossed tin tacker sign, American Art Works, Coshocton, Ohio, c. 1920. USA, 17 1/2" x 17 3/4". Rarity 10. $550

Porcelain sign, Beaver Enamel Co. Elwood City, Pennsylvania, c. 1920. As rare as it is large, this big sign is usually found in this kind of condition or restored. USA, 60" x 30". *Collection Brian E Harto.* Rarity 8. $750

Porcelain sign, with great graphics of Bibendum sleeping in the tire, 1920s. The quality of this sign is stunning, a vertical version of this sign also exists. USA, 17 3/4" x 59 3/4". Rarity 8. $1,200

Domed porcelain sign, c. 1920, with nice vignette in the corner depicting the "Nunc est Bibendum" poster. A very plain sign, but nevertheless early and rare. Milano, Italy, 25 3/4" x 17 1/2". *Collection Etienne Levillain.* Rarity 8. $400

Tin sign, most likely made by Louis Cannard or De Andreis, c. 1930. This sign is only a portion of a shelving system used as a tire rack in service stations for decades. Usually 2 or 3 shelves per unit, they were modular and came in different sizes, the side panels were similar signs but without the Bibendum's head. 5" x 33 1/2". As shown: Rarity 6. $150; Complete rack: Rarity 8. $750

Small double-sided tin sign, Louis Cannard, 1920s. Designed to be attached to larger double-sided Michelin signs, it advertises that maps could be purchased in addition to tires and tubes. This sign can be found with different manufacturers including Cannard, De Andreis, and Revon. A large find, manufactured by Cannard, turned up a few years ago. France, 13 3/4" x 8". Rarity 6. $30

Heavily embossed tin sign, c. 1940. Originally mounted on the side of a wood-burning stove, manufactured by Michelin during World War II. Complete cast iron stove, *Collection Gilles Dutto*. Rarity 8. $275; Sign only, France, 4 3/4" round. Rarity 8. $225

Tin dispenser for tire repair patches, Decalco R. Senecaut, Paris, c. 1920. This counter display is incredibly rare. France, 15" x 7". Rarity 10. $700

Double-sided embossed tin sign, Louis Cannard, 1930. There is a 1928 version of this sign showing a different tire. France, 29 1/2" x 29 1/2". As shown: Rarity 7. $500; 1928 version: Rarity 8. $550

Double-sided embossed tin sign, Imprimeto, Paris, 1935. From a group of three signs that look relatively the same, this is by far the best of the bunch because of its smaller size, much higher embossing, and just all around better quality. It is also the rarest version…of course! *Collection Gilles Dutto,* France, 23 1/2" x 23 1/4". Rarity 9. $550

Tin tire holder, 1930s. Very rarely seen, this makes a great display when matched with a Michelin tire of the same vintage. France. *Collection Martin Burger.* Rarity 9.

Double-sided embossed tin sign, De Andreis, 1934. A great sign, it is completely embossed with brighter colors than usual. Six of these signs were found NOS in the mid 1980s, and all found their places in collections rather quickly. They are now rarely found in any condition. France, 23 1/2" x 23 1/2". Rarity 8. $800

Beveled mirror in original wooden frame, 1930s. UK. 28" x 19". *Collection David Ralph.* Rarity 9. $250

Porcelain sign by Chromo Wolverhampton, 1930s. There are unusual three-dimensional graphics on this very rare, single-sided sign, meant to assure customers that they were buying a product manufactured in England. UK, 44 1/2" x 25". Rarity 10. $800

Porcelain sign, 1930s. Rarely seen. UK, 57 1/2" x 15 3/4". Rarity 9. $600

Porcelain sign, 1930s. With graphics practically identical to the UK version, this sign was made in Argentina, 59" x 15 3/4". Rarity 7. $500

Porcelain sign by M. Maumus, 1930s. A very desirable sign, the lack of text makes this sign appeal to collectors regardless of their language, but it is primarily sought after because the multiple Bibendums on a sign are very rarely seen. Argentina, 15 3/4 x 71". Rarity 9. $1,000

Tin sign, 1940s. Very scarce tin sign advertising motorcycle tires. Spain, 13 1/4" x 19 1/4". Rarity 10

Aluminum sign, 1940s. F.I.L.A.M Milano. Very scarce, this is a smaller version than its Spanish counterpart. Italy, 7 3/4" x 9 3/4". Rarity 10

Tin sign, De Andreis, 1940s. This very scarce tin sign with unusual graphics was also made as a cardboard sign. France, 13 1/2" x 9 1/2". Rarity 9. $550

Die-cut tin sign, c. 1948. Great, unusual graphics of Bibendum holding a sign. Die-cut signs are very popular among advertising collectors and this one is a favorite. Belgium. *Collection Martin Burger.* Rarity 9

Tin embossed push plate, 1949. Wiart, Belgium 4 3/4" x 14 1/2". Rarity 8. $300

Tin push plate, Ets. Chambon, France, 1949. 10 1/4" x 4 3/4". Rarity 8. $250

Aluminum push-plate, c. 1940. This seldom seen sign is prone to bubbling and peeling of the paint due to the material used. UK, 14 1/2" x 4 1/2". Rarity 8. $250

Porcelain sign, 1947. Belgium, 23 3/4" x 15 3/4". *Collection Etienne Levillain*. Rarity 9. $700

Shelf edge strips. From top to bottom: 1940s, UK, 19" x 2 1/4", Rarity 6. $75; UK. 18 1/2" x 1 1/4" 1940s, UK, Rarity 5, $50; 1950s, France, 18 1/2" x 1", Rarity 5, $30; 1960s, France, 18 1/2" x 1", Rarity 4, $20

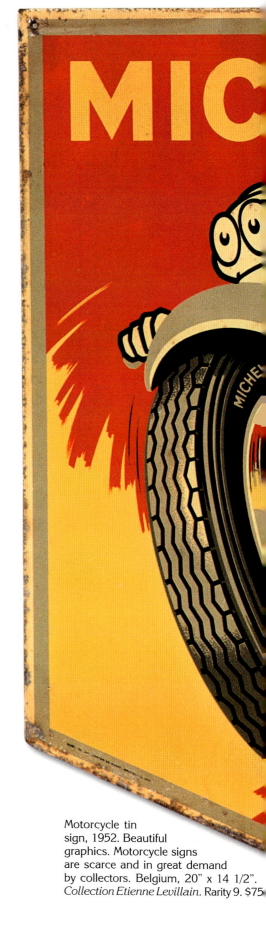

Motorcycle tin sign, 1952. Beautiful graphics. Motorcycle signs are scarce and in great demand by collectors. Belgium, 20" x 14 1/2". *Collection Etienne Levillain*. Rarity 9. $75

Double-sided flange sign, Cellulocolor, Argenteuil, 1952. The drop shadow behind Bib possibly signifies that the tire advertised is for trucks. France, 21 5/8" x 16". *Collection Patrick Jehanno.* Rarity 8. $250

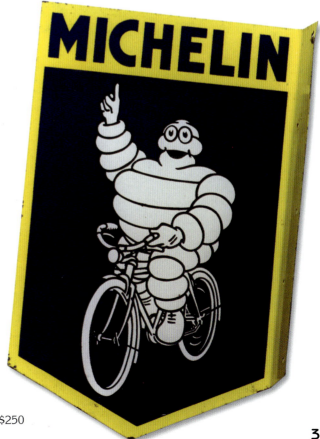

Tin flange sign, 1948. Belgium. Rarity 9. $250

Porcelain sign, 1948. Very desirable. Belgium, 18 3/4" x 11 3/4". Rarity 8. $500

Porcelain sign, 1950s. Very scarce service sign, it is very desirable due to the out of the ordinary colors and graphics. Bilbao, Spain. 31 1/2" x 26 3/4". Rarity 9. $450

Porcelain truck door sign, c. 1950. Italy, 19" x 17". Rarity 9. $200

Porcelain sign for truck tires, Art France, 1955. 17 1/2" x 15". *Collection Patrick Jehanno*. Rarity 7. $225

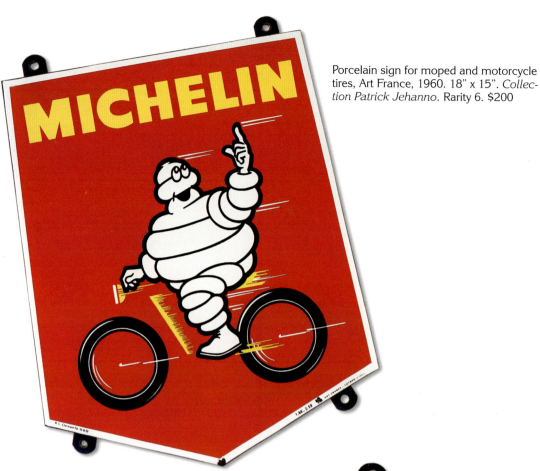

Porcelain sign for moped and motorcycle tires, Art France, 1960. 18" x 15". *Collection Patrick Jehanno*. Rarity 6. $200

Porcelain sign, EAS (Emaillerie Alsacienne Strasbourg), 1961. This sign was produced for many years and was also available in different sizes. France, 18" x 15". *Collection Patrick Jehanno*. Rarity 5. $125

Porcelain sign for tractor tires, EAS (Emaillerie Alsacienne Strasbourg), 1955. France, 24" x 18". *Collection Patrick Jehanno.* Rarity 5. $200

Porcelain sign for tractor tires, Art France-Laynes, 1960. France, 31 1/2" x 26 3/4". Rarity 6. $200

Scarce aluminum sign destined to be mounted on heavy machinery, c. 1950. France, 4 3/4" x 3 1/4". Rarity 10. $85

Porcelain sign, 1950s. This sign was used both on front of buildings and on sides of service trucks. Belgium, 23 5/8" x 78 3/4". Rarity 8. $350

Porcelain sign, c. 1950-1960. This sign was used for many years often found with graphics of different types of tires. Belgium, 31 1/2" x 25 1/2". Rarity 7. $250

Porcelain sign, EAS, c. 1950-1960. This very scarce sign was found in Taiwan but was manufactured in France. Unknown to collectors in Europe, here again is another example of a sign made specifically for export to another part of the world. Note the absence of text. France, 57 1/2" x 23 1/2". Rarity 10. $700

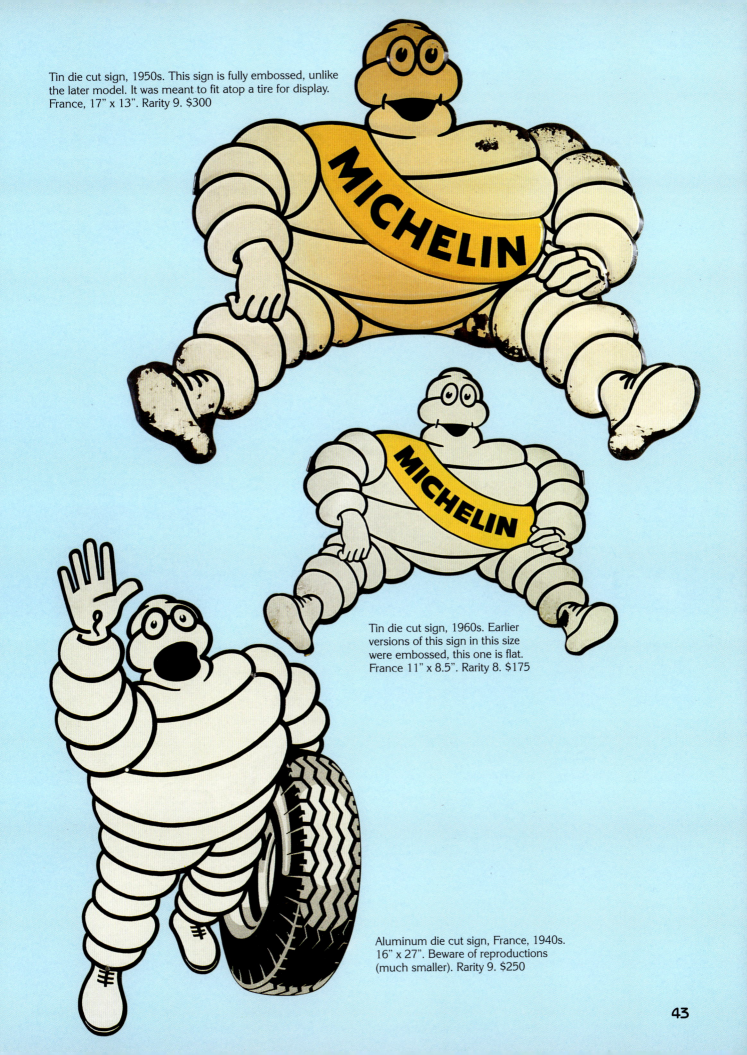

Tin die cut sign, 1950s. This sign is fully embossed, unlike the later model. It was meant to fit atop a tire for display. France, 17" x 13". Rarity 9. $300

Tin die cut sign, 1960s. Earlier versions of this sign in this size were embossed, this one is flat. France 11" x 8.5". Rarity 8. $175

Aluminum die cut sign, France, 1940s. 16" x 27". Beware of reproductions (much smaller). Rarity 9. $250

Tin map counter display, 1956. The sign itself is seen more often on its own; the complete display isn't easily obtainable. France, 21 1/2' x 16". Rarity 8. $275

Die-cut aluminum sidewalk sign, 1960s, shown here mounted on its original support, which is usually removed. The sign itself is made of 5 signs riveted together. France, approximately 31" tall. *Collection Pascal Eveno. Rarity* 7. $300

Top: Cartes et Guides (maps and guides) tin sign, France, 1957. 16 1/2" x 3 1/2". Rarity 6. $150. **Bottom:** Service Michelin aluminum sign, France, 1940s. 23 1/2" x 4". Rarity 8. $175

Ceramic tiles, 1950s. These great tiles were designed to decorate the interiors of garages in Spain. Beware of reproductions that are just blue tiles with Bibs silk screened on top. Check for a complete glaze over both background and Bibs to insure that they were kiln-fired after the silk screening. As shown: Rarity 8. $700; Individual tiles: Rarity 6. $40

Masonite sign, c. 1945. This sign exists in as many variations as there were types of tires, and many colors variants as well. It was installed inside a tire as a store display. France, 25" diameter. *Collection Damian J Cessario.* Rarity 6. $125

Tin sign designed by Raymond Savignac, France, 1966. *Courtesy Tomonari Sakurai "Grays."* 31 1/2" x 23 1/2". Rarity 7. $150

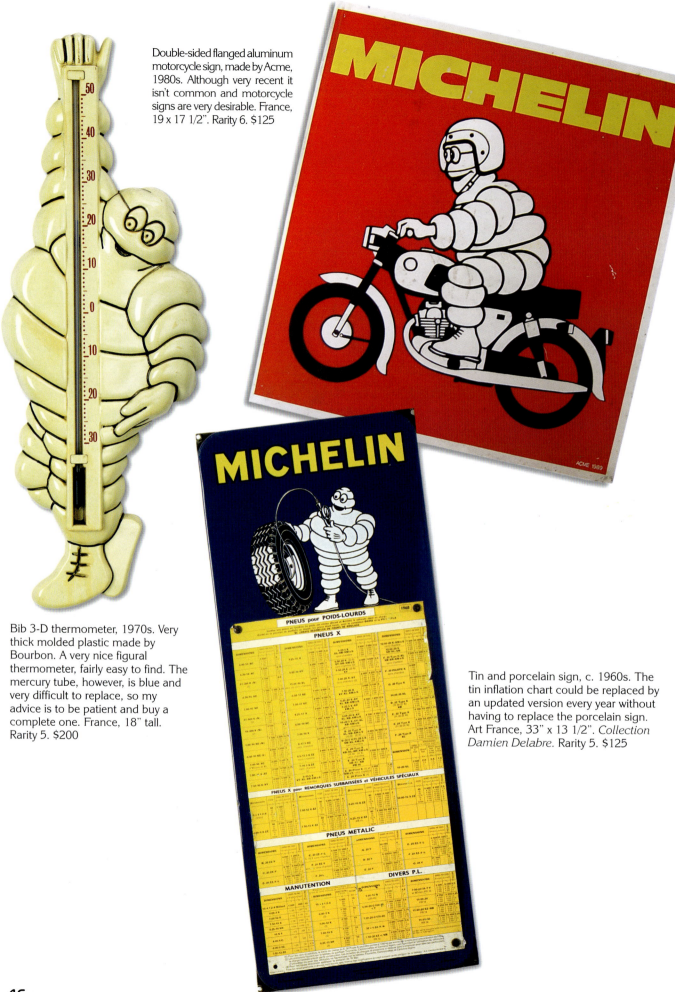

Double-sided flanged aluminum motorcycle sign, made by Acme, 1980s. Although very recent it isn't common and motorcycle signs are very desirable. France, 19 x 17 1/2". Rarity 6. $125

Bib 3-D thermometer, 1970s. Very thick molded plastic made by Bourbon. A very nice figural thermometer, fairly easy to find. The mercury tube, however, is blue and very difficult to replace, so my advice is to be patient and buy a complete one. France, 18" tall. Rarity 5. $200

Tin and porcelain sign, c. 1960s. The tin inflation chart could be replaced by an updated version every year without having to replace the porcelain sign. Art France, 33" x 13 1/2". *Collection Damien Delabre.* Rarity 5. $125

Double-sided light-up sign, Dualite, Ohio, 1970s. Plastic and aluminum. USA 36" x 12" *Collection Patrick Jehanno. Rarity* 6. $75

Aluminum sign, 1980s. This came as a single-sided sign and as a double-sided flange sign. France, 19" x 17 1/2". Single: Rarity 5. $40; flange: Rarity 5. $70

Double-sided light up sign, France, 1970s to 1980s. 32" x 27". *Collection Patrick Jehanno. Rarity* 8. $250

Chapter Three
Tins, Containers, and Tools

Garage tin repair outfit, code "Paragon," G. De Andreis, Marseille, France, 1928. 16" x 8" closed. This tin is often thought to be a first aid kit from the nature of its graphics, it was hung on the walls of garages and gas stations ready for action, containing all the necessary tools to repair a puncture. It had wide distribution and isn't difficult to find, however finding one in this condition, with all of its original contents is miraculous! A brown version, code "Paradis," also exists. Empty: Rarity 6. $200. Full: Rarity 10. $750

Talcum powder tin, code "Nuance." France, 1928. 3" x 3". Rarity 9. $100

Mastic tin, code "Formosa." France, 1928. 3" x 2". Rarity 9. $50

Solution tin, code "Parapet." France, c. 1930. 3" x 3". Rarity 9. $100

Solution tin code "Parapet." France, c.1930. 3" x 3". Rarity 9 $100

Dissolution tin, code "Parapet." France, 1928.
3" x 3". Rarity 9. $100

Solution tin, code "Patine." France, 1928.
3" x 3". Rarity 9. $100

Dissolution tin code "Parapet." France, c. 1925. 4 3/4" x 3". *Collection Gilles Dutto*. Rarity 9. $100

Filler tin with paper label, code "Falcon." France, c. 1910. 2" x 1 1/4". Rarity 9. $60

Cement tin code "Tirbo," Milltown, New Jersey, c. 1915. 2" x 2". Rarity 9. $35

Mastic tin. France, c. 1910. 3 1/2" x 2 3/4". *Collection Gilles Dutto. Rarity* 9. $85

Mastic tin with paper label, code "Tokay." Milltown, New Jersey, 1922. 2" x 2". Rarity 9. $75

Wooden slide-top toolbox, code "Tidy," shown as it would have been sold to automobilists. The thin yet solid box was perfectly designed to fit under a driver's seat without being obstructive. It contained all of the tools necessary to repair a puncture, with the exception of a crick. The lid is marked " L'indispensable Michelin montage et reparations" translates to "The indispensable Michelin mounting and repairs." France, c. 1920. 17 1/4" x 3 3/4" x 2". Empty: Rarity 5. $25; full as shown: Rarity 9. $350

Scarce wooden slide-top toolbox. Another example but this one is earlier and American, no interior compartment. USA, c. 1910. 12 1/2" x 3" x 2". Rarity 9. $75

Filler tin, code "Falcon." France, c. 1920. 2" x 1 1/4". Rarity 7. $40

Filler tin, code "Focalis." France, c. 1920. 2" x 1 1/4". Rarity 7. $40

Talcum powder tubes, left to right: Tin, code "Naviger," France, c.1910, 5 1/2" x 1 1/4", Rarity 9, $75; Tin, code "Impair," Milltown, New Jersey, c.1915, 5 1/2" x 1 1/4", Rarity 9, $100; Cardboard, code "Naviger," France, c.1918, 5" x 1 1/4", Rarity 9, $100; Tin, code "Naviger," France, c.1920, 5 1/2" x 1 1/4", Rarity 8, $125

Rubber cement tubes, code "Panic" (2 variations), "Paralipse," and "Reras." France, c. 1925 to 1960s. 2 1/2" to 4 3/4" long. Rarity 8. $35 each

Rubber cement tin, code "Parade." France, c. 1930 3" x 3". Rarity 8. $100

Rubber cement container in black Bakelite, code "Parade," cold dissolution, France, c. 1930. 3 1/4" x 3 1/4". Rarity 6. $75. Also exists as code "Peata" in brown Bakelite, hot dissolution. Rarity 8. $100

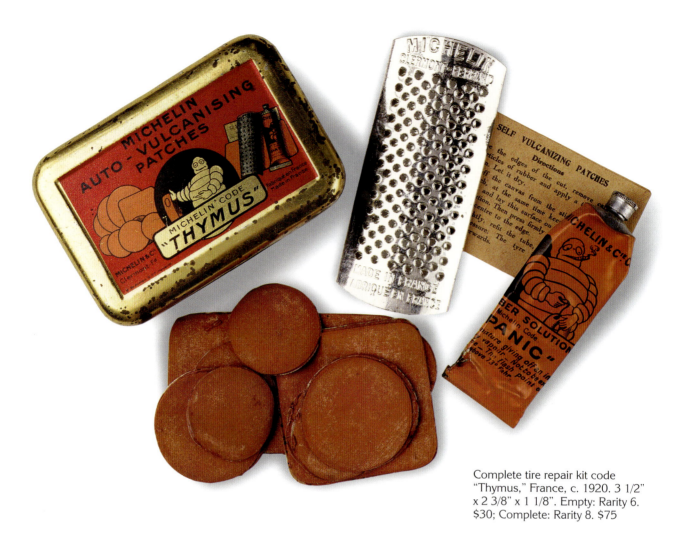

Complete tire repair kit code "Thymus," France, c. 1920. 3 1/2" x 2 3/8" x 1 1/8". Empty: Rarity 6. $30; Complete: Rarity 8. $75

Tire repair kit code "Thyrse." I believe the blue tube of glue is a replacement, the original is more likely to be orange. France, c. 1920. 2 3/4" x 1 5/8" x 5/8". Empty: Rarity 6. $20. Complete: Rarity 8. $50

Universal repair kit tin. Shown here with instructions. USA, c. 1915. 6" x 4" x 4". *Courtesy Milltown Museum, Milltown Historical Society.* Rarity 9. $35

Puncture repair kit tin. USA, c. 1910. 4 1/2" x 3 1/4" x 1 1/4". *Collection Brian E. Harto.* Rarity 10. $35

Puncture repair kit tin, Milltown, New Jersey, c. 1910. 3" x 2" x 1". Rarity 9. $35

Puncture repair kit tin, code "Thalo," France, c. 1910. 3" x 2" x 3/4". Rarity 7. $15

Tire patch tin, code "Fissure," France, c. 1930. 3 1/2" x 3 1/4" x 3/4". Rarity 9. $125

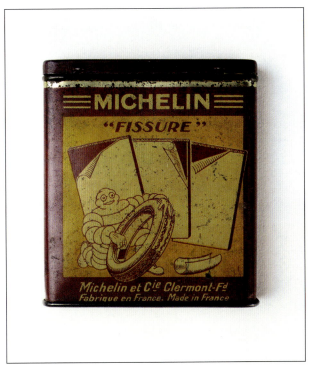

Valve tin, code "Lucrative," France, 1928. 1 1/8"x 1 1/8" x 1/4". Rarity 4. $5

Patches tins. Code "Pagaie," 2 1/4" x 1 5/8"; code "Precaution," 2 1/4" x 2"; code "Panelle," 1 1/2" x 1 5/8" France, c. 1930. Rarity 6. $15 to $50

Tire patches tin, code "Pacite," France, c. 1930. 4" x 2 1/2" x 1 1/2". Rarity 7. $75

Truck tire patches tin, code "Prediction," France, c. 1930. 4" x 1 3/4" x 2 1/2". Rarity 7. $75

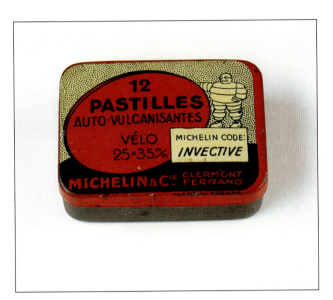

Patches tin, code "Invective," France, c. 1930. 2" x 1 1/2" x 5/8". Rarity 8. $35

Patches tin, code "Invective," France, c. 1930. 1 5/8" x 1/2". Rarity 8. $50

Grease tin, code "Tigre," France, c. 1940. 4 1/2" x 3 1/2". Rarity 8. $125

Box for bicycle tube. UK, c. 1950. 3 7/8" x 3 7/8" x 2". Rarity 8. $30

Cardboard box for 12 tubes of rubber cement, code "Pelor," France, c. 1940. 3 1/2" x 2 3/4" x 1 1/2". Rarity 9. $50

Puncture repair tin, code "Reruc," France, c. 1940.
3 1/4" x 2 1/4" x 3/4". Rarity 7. $30

Pressure gauges with tins, France, c. 1900.
2 3/4" x 2 3/4" x 2". Rarity 8. $150

Pressure gauge tins, France, c. 1900. 4" x 3" x 1 3/4". Rarity 9. Empty. $100; with gauge. $200

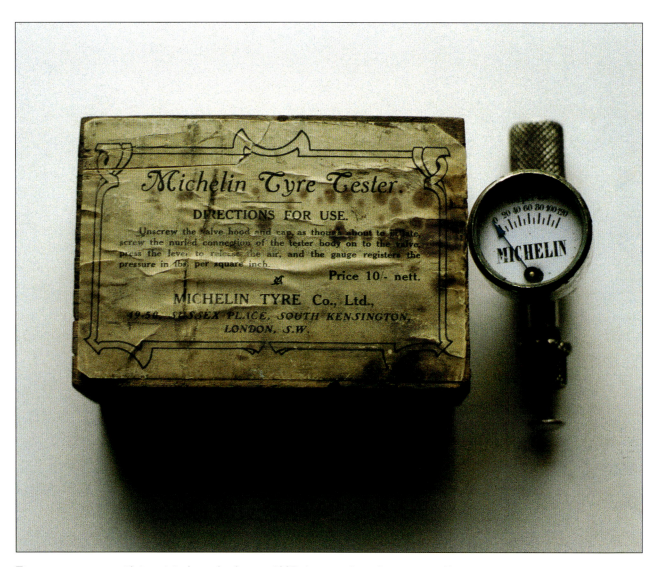

Tire pressure gauge with its original wooden box, c. 1905. A very early and rare gauge. Even rarer is the paper label on the box, with a rarely seen "Sussex Place" address, Michelin's office in London before the opening of the Bibendum building in 1911. UK, Box 4 1/2" x 3" x 2". Rarity 10; gauge 4" x 2 1/2". *Collection David Ralph.* Rarity 9

Pressure gauge with tin and instructions, code "Flora," France, 1930. 3" x 1 3/4" x 1". Rarity 8. $75 as shown

Pressure gauge with tin and instructions, code "Flora," France, 1929. 3" x 1 3/4" x 1". Rarity 8 complete as shown. $100

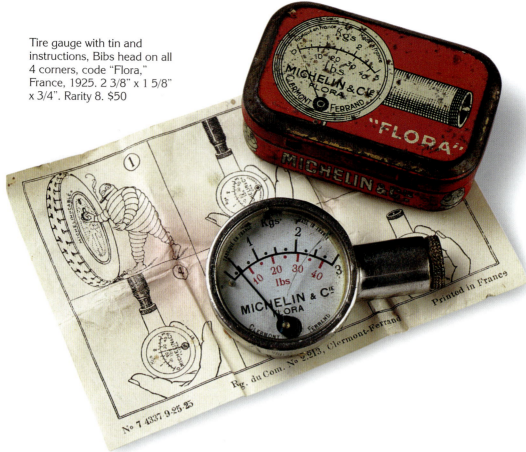

Tire gauge with tin and instructions, Bibs head on all 4 corners, code "Flora," France, 1925. 2 3/8" x 1 5/8" x 3/4". Rarity 8. $50

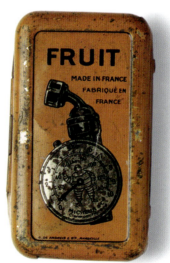

Pressure gauge with tin code "Fruit," France, 1930. 3" x 1 3/4" x 1". Rarity 9. $100

Tire gauge with tin, Bibs head on all 4 corners, code "Femur," France, 1925. 2 3/8" x 1 5/8" x 3/4". *Collection Robert J Harrington.* Rarity 8. $50

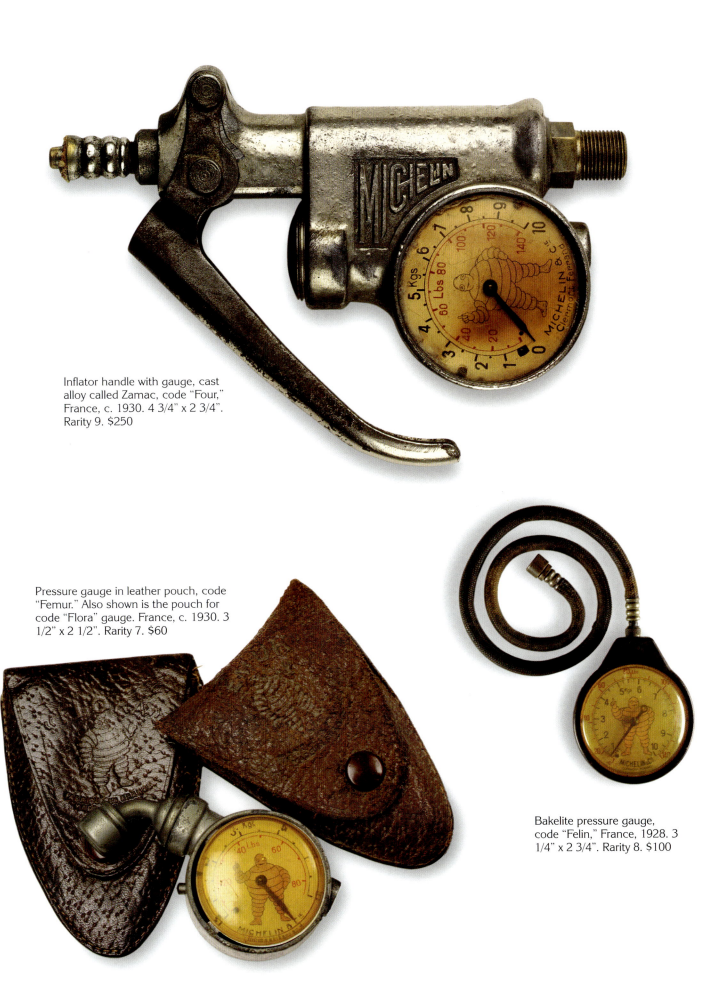

Inflator handle with gauge, cast alloy called Zamac, code "Four," France, c. 1930. 4 3/4" x 2 3/4". Rarity 9. $250

Pressure gauge in leather pouch, code "Femur." Also shown is the pouch for code "Flora" gauge. France, c. 1930. 3 1/2" x 2 1/2". Rarity 7. $60

Bakelite pressure gauge, code "Felin," France, 1928. 3 1/4" x 2 3/4". Rarity 8. $100

67

Bakelite pressure gauge, code "Factum," France, c. 1930. 6 1/2" x 3" x 1 1/4". Rarity 8. $75

Tin die-cut sign for Schrader pressure gauge, c. 1915. This tin lithographed sign is the perfect display solution for an otherwise hard to show gauge. USA, 5 3/4" diameter. *Collection Robert J Harrington. Rarity* 9. $150

Nickel-plated pressure gauge by Schrader's Son, Brooklyn, New York, c. 1910, 2 1/2" x 3/4". Rarity 5. $40

Nickel-plated valve cap, Milltown, New Jersey, c. 1910. 2 3/4". Rarity 7. $50

Valve in envelope, code "Lucifer," France, c. 1910. 2 1/2" x 1 3/4". Rarity 7. $15

Nickel-plated figural screwdriver, France, c. 1920. 2 3/8" x 1 3/4". Rarity 9. $200

Chromed figural screwdriver, France, c. 1950. 1 3/4" x 1 1/4". Rarity 6. $25

Envelope for rubber patches, c. 1915. This would have been found in the Michelin Universal Repair kit and a wooden slide top toolbox. USA, 3 1/8" x 5 1/2". *Collection Robert J Harrington. Rarity* 9. $30

Tin map display box, France, 12 1/2" x 5 1/2". *Collection Damian J Cessario*. Rarity 9. $150

Rare wooden box for the elusive compressed air bottle. France, c. 1900. 8 1/2" x 6 1/2" x 3". *Collection David Ralph*. Rarity 9. $200

Display tins for maps, France, 12 1/2" x 5 1/2". From top to bottom: advertising "Stop" tires, 1935, Rarity 9, $150; 1949, Rarity 8, $100; 1954, Rarity 7, $75

Very scarce wooden shipping crate, c. 1910. Both sides are printed with a very early Bibendum, USA, 45 1/2" x 19" x 14 1/2". Rarity 10. $450

Chapter Four
Clocks and Calendars

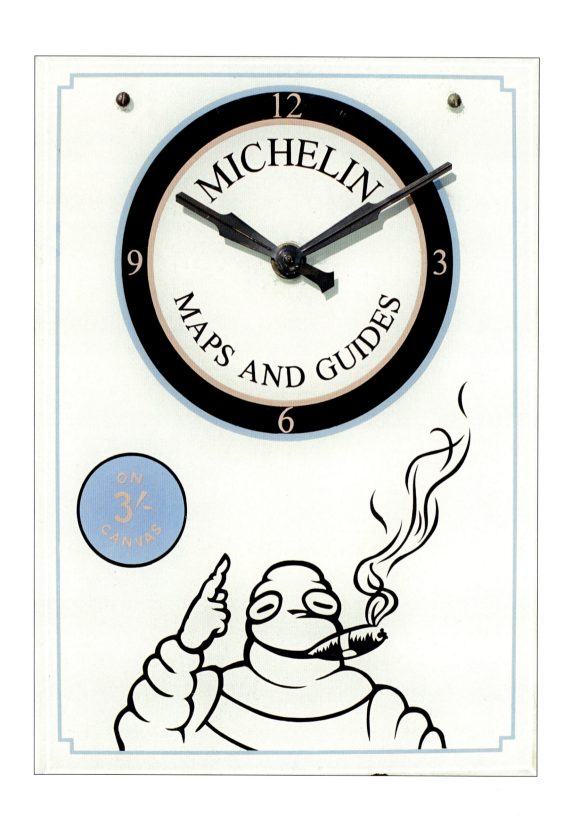

Very scarce 3 1/2" diameter clock made to resemble tortoise shell, with deeply engraved graphics. France, c. 1920. Rarity 10. $700

A stunning and unusual piece, this perpetual calendar is a rare find. Shown here in its original box, it illustrates father time failing to damage an unfazed Bibendum. Made to look like tortoise shell with deep gold-filled engravings. France, c. 1920. 4 1/2" x 2 7/8". Rarity 9. $700

This nice desk clock, also made to resemble tortoise shell with gold-filled details, is much easier to obtain than the perpetual calendar of the same style. France, c. 1920. 4 1/2" x 3". Rarity 7. $350

Dashboard clocks ran on 6 volts, hence the graphics of Bib holding lightning bolts and the unusual design of the clocks hands. Swiss made, late 1920s to early 1930s, 4" diameter, two equally rare examples shown. White face clock: *Collection Damian J Cessario.* Rarity 9. $350

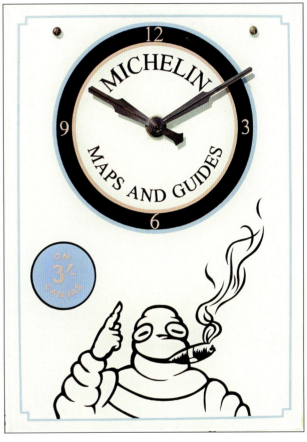

Very scarce 1920s large glass wall clock, this one is electric and hangs on a chain from the top, deeply etched and reverse painted. It has a small round vignette advertising the maps on canvas. British made, 14 1/2" x 9 1/2" Great piece!. Rarity 10.

Electric travel clock with leather casing, late 1920s. The clock opens and reveals the mechanism and the battery compartment. It can be found in green, brown, and burgundy. The leather handle is generally broken or missing as it is on this example. France, 4" x 3" x 2 1/2". Rarity 7. $250

Alabaster clock, with all the graphics deeply etched into the stone. Made by Angelus, England, 1950. 6 1/2" x 5" x 2". Rarity 10. $250.

Clock, reverse painted glass, made by Smiths (manufacturer of automobile clocks), England, late 1940s. 7 1/2" x 4 1/2". *Collection Damian J Cessario. Rarity* 10. $250

Flasher light-up clock, plastic and tin, made by Dualite Ohio, USA, 1970s. 17" x 14". Rarity 6. $75

Chapter Five
Smalls

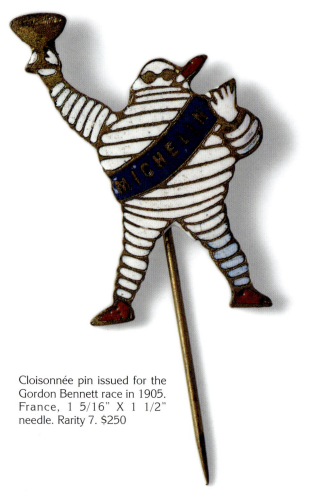

Cloisonnée pin issued for the Gordon Bennett race in 1905. France, 1 5/16" X 1 1/2" needle. Rarity 7. $250

This 1905 bronze brooch, very scarce, was also issued for the Gordon Bennett race, however it is practically impossible to find one of these. France, 1 1/16" diameter. Rarity 9. $400

Cloisonnée over bronze pin with very sharp and crisp details, c. 1910. This is the only one I have ever come across. It was most likely made at the occasion of a race or the inauguration of the Turin factory in 1906. Italy, 1 3/16" tall. Rarity 10. $200

Silver-plated bronze brooch, c. 1910. The most common of the early pins, this still makes a nice addition for a collection, and it is easily obtainable. France, 1 1/8" diameter. Rarity 6. $125

This cloisonnée brooch, c. 1920, is very tough to find in nice condition. Some are just marked "Michelin." Made in Czechoslovakia, 1 3/16" diameter. Rarity 8. $400

Cloisonnée brooch, smaller version, possibly earlier than the preceding example and with sharper details. Made in Czechoslovakia, for export. 1 1/16" diameter. Rarity 8. $400

Amazing pencil clip, 1920s. Nickel-plated bronze. The Bibendum smoking his cigar is identical to the one found on the 1920 note pad and leather key holder. A very important piece for the American collector. USA, 1 1/8" x 7/8". Rarity 10

Very scarce salesman cloisonnée boutonnière, Greenduck Company, Chicago, c. 1907. Certainly among the first advertising items made in the United States after Michelin's arrival in 1907. USA, tiny 9/16". Rarity 10. $200

Mother-of-pearl brooch, c. 1920. Deeply engraved, England, 1 3/4" diameter. *Collection Damian J Cessario.* Rarity 10

Commemorative sterling silver pendant, 1937. Made for the 10th anniversary of the Stoke-on-Trent factory in England, each medal was engraved with the name of an employee present during those 10 years. England, 1 3/8" diameter. Rarity 8. $175

Cloisonnée boutonnière, G. Moret, Paris, France, 1940s. 1 3/16" diameter. Rarity 9. $150

Wooden sewing kit, 1920s. This particular one is a salesman sample; it is not known whether it ever went into production for Michelin. It is the only example I have ever run across. USA, 3 1/8" x 1 1/2". Rarity 10

Cloisonnée key chain, France, c. 1960. 1 1/2". Rarity 6. $10

Hand-tinted glass slide, Tom Phillips Slide Co. Chicago, 1920s. This type of slide was used during intermissions in movie theaters to advertise local businesses. USA, 4" x 3 1/4". Rarity 10. $200

Printer's blocks, c. 1920. These die-cut copper plates are mounted on wood blocks, used to print anything from map covers to brochures and letterheads. The larger, older models are very desirable. USA. Rarity 8. $50-150

Another great group of printing blocks, c. 1920. USA. *Collection Martin Burger.* Rarity 8. $50-$150

Very scarce deck of playing cards, c. 1920. Sides of the box marked "Michelin Tires" and "Michelin Tubes." USA 3 1/2" x 2 1/2". Rarity 9. $200

Another very scarce deck of playing cards, c. 1920. This one advertises the "Universal Tread tire." USA, 3 1/2" x 2 1/2". Rarity 9. $200

Leather billfold, c. 1920. USA 8 1/2" x 3 3/4". Rarity 8. $75

Leather billfold, c. 1920. USA, 9" x 4 3/4" opened. *Collection John Collins.* Rarity 8. $75

Great leather key holder, c. 1920. Two leather, overlapping flaps keep the keys together. They are held shut by a pressure button embossed with Bib's head smoking his cigar. USA, 3 1/2" x 2 1/4". Rarity 9. $150

Leather business card holder, c. 1920. Also has a Bib's head pressure button. USA, 7 7/8" x 1 7/8" opened. Rarity 9. $100

Leather note pad, c. 1920. Each page has a watermark of Bibendum standing and smoking his cigar. USA, 4 3/8" x 2 5/8". Rarity 10. $125

Leather pouch for tire gauge, 1930s. It is embossed with the effigy of Bibendum and marked "Flora;" also seen marked "Femur." France, 3 1/2" x 2 1/2". Rarity 7. $50

Matchbook and matchbook holder, 1920s, leather with a nickel-plated insert to hold a book of matches. I was fortunate to have found this one still containing its original matchbook, as I have never seen the matches elsewhere. The other example shown has faux sharkskin. USA 2 1/4" x 1 3/4'. Without matchbook: Rarity 9. $125; Complete: Rarity 9. $200

Nickel-plated lighters, c. 1920. Deep embossing of the Bibendum lighting his cigar. Back is marked "Michelin." Two versions are shown. These great lighters are often found on the market, but usually the plating is worn down to the brass. France, 2 5/8" x 1 1/4". Rarity 7. $150

Balboa lighter with great graphics of Bibendum deeply cut into the side of the lighter, 1950s. A really nice item. *Collection Martin Burger.* Rarity 9. $85

Ronson lighter in its presentation box, 1960s. *Collection Martin Burger.* Rarity 9. $75

Ceramic ashtray, c. 1950. In my opinion, this is the best Michelin ashtray, both in design and its color scheme of turquoise and ivory. Deep, sharp details, very high quality. France, 4 1/2" tall. Rarity 9. $300

Many color variations were made on the 3 different styles of ceramic ashtrays; here is a burgundy example identical to the turquoise. Note the absence of wording on the base.

Ceramic ashtray, late 1950s. This scarce style variation has a solid base with a wavy edge. This version is notorious for breaking at the ankles. France, 4 1/4" tall. Red base *Collection Peggy and Ed Strauss*. Yellow base *Collection Patrick Jehanno*. Rarity 8. $200

Bakelite ashtray, 1940s. A very common item but a very well designed and realized piece. Also exists with a black and a green Bakelite base. England, 4 3/4" x 5 1/4". Rarity 5. $100; Green base: Rarity 8. $200 Note: Beware of exact ceramic reproductions with a green base and white Bib. There is also a polished aluminum cast reproduction that has the merit of being attractive.

Ceramic ashtray, c. 1960-1970. I only know this later version in two colors, burgundy and green. It is often marked with a dealer's name on the base. Much lighter than earlier versions, and the details aren't as sharp. Belgium, 4 1/2" tall. Rarity 6. $150

Black base ashtray. Identical to the English version but made of plastic not Bakelite. Marked at the bottom made in USA. Date of manufacture unknown, however, dozens of these turned up at antique shows in the late 1980s in their original boxes, never assembled, and all wrapped in 1983 newspapers, leading me to believe that they may have been a 1980s production. USA, 4 3/4" x 5 1/4". Rarity 4. $75 Note: When in doubt, best way to establish whether an object is plastic or Bakelite, is to heat it up by rubbing it vigorously with your knuckles or finger tips. The Bakelite will emit a strong, distinctive odor; the plastic will not.

Desk penholder, 1920s. The only one I have ever seen. UK, 9" x 5". *Collection David Ralph*. Rarity 10

This marble plaque was made to look like an opened mid-1920s Michelin guide. It would have been fastened to the façade of a building. This is the only example I have ever seen. France, 11" x 8 1/2" x 2 1/2". *Collection David Ralph*. Rarity 10

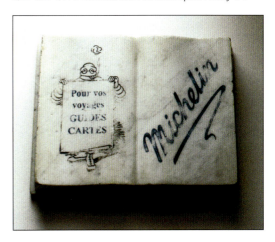

Bakelite cup, 1930s. A scarce item, it was part of a whole Bakelite desk set. UK, 3 3/4" x 2 3/4". *Collection David Ralph*. Rarity 9. $125

Bakelite lamp, 1930s. This great example still has its original glass shade, with Bibendums climbing all around the stem, a gorgeous piece. UK, 18" x 7 1/2". *Collection David Ralph*. Rarity 9

Fireman's helmet from Michelin's own fire department, most likely from the Clermont-Ferrand Factory, c. 1910. *Collection Martin Burger.* Rarity 9

Amazing c.1915 felt pennant, designed to hang in the windows of service stations and showrooms. A very scarce and important item. USA, 11 1/2" x 28". *Courtesy Milltown Museum, Milltown Historical Society.* Rarity 10

Felt station attendant hat, c. 1920. A very scarce item, this turned up in beautiful unused condition. USA, 11 1/2" x 5". Rarity 10

Die-cast Micheline rail car, c. 1930, made in France by Louis Roussy. This fantastic 20 volts electric rail car was based on the real Micheline, the first rail car to ride on tires. Created in 1929 by Michelin, they were introduced to the public in 1931. Two are still in use today in Madagascar. France, 15 3/4" x 3 1/2" x 2 1/8". Rarity 9. $ 850

Back of felt station attendant hat on page 94.

Deviating a little bit from Bibendum, but I am sure you'll forgive me, who could resist this large tin Alpha Romeo wind up racer, made by the French firm CIJ in the 1920s. They came in a variety of colors and not always on Michelin tires. This orange version looks most appropriate to fit in a Michelin collection. France, 20" Long. Rarity 8

95

Chapter Six
Figural Displays

In the 1920s plaster statues of Bibendum were distributed to tire dealers. Designed to stand guard and welcome customers at the entrance of showrooms and service stations, they often fell victim to Mother Nature's rain and snow. Some more fortunate ones were displayed indoors, either by the counters or as window displays. They were originally painted in a light grey for the body, yellow lettering on a blue sash, brown boots, blue base, and, occasionally, flesh tone hands. Another variation with a white body and a black outline separating each tire was improperly dismissed as restored for years, but it is more likely that they were refurbished by Michelin in the late 1920s as few have turned up with identical paint and surface scratching revealed the original grey underneath. Several 1920s photos have also turned up showing this exact variant. Many statues were, however, often repainted by their owners, who were not always particular about the colors used. Those represent the majority of the examples found today. They usually have a great patina and, in my opinion, are best kept this way rather than restored.

Large papier maché figure, c. 1920. A very impressive piece, this example has survived with its original paint. The base reads "Michelin Casings and Tubes." The word "Casing" was abandoned and replaced by the word "Tire" in the 1920s. USA, 36 1/2" tall. *Collection Robert J Harrington. Rarity 9*

Plaster statue, c. 1920. Instead of wearing a Michelin sash, this version of the statue has "Michelin Tires and Tubes" marked on the base. Also note that the arms are in the opposite position from the other plaster version. The example shown has its original paint and goggles. USA, 32" x 16". *Collection Peggy and Ed Strauss. Rarity 10*

Plaster statue, c. 1920. This highly sought-after version has the familiar sash going across its chest, marked "Michelin Tires." There are no markings on the base. The great example shown here has its original metal goggles. The sash, legs, boots, and base have their original paint, while the upper body and head have a very old repaint. USA, 32" x 16". Rarity 9

Another great example of a very desirable plaster statue.

Cast iron figure, c. 1928. Also from a large compressor, this one made by Worthington. This example appears to have its original paint, but it is very difficult to tell for sure as the compressors were serviced and refurbished by Michelin over the years. Note that a cast iron Bibendum made for a Luchard compressor will not fit on a compressor made by Worthington and vise versa. France, 14" x 10". Rarity 8. $400

Cast iron figure, c. 1928. This was on the large compressor made by Luchard. It is the larger of the two versions. This great example has completely lost its paint, giving it a wonderful primitive look. France, 14 1/2" x 12". Rarity 8. $400

1928 air compressor with figural cast iron Bibendum, code "Force." Two different models exist, one made by Worthington and the other by Luchard. Widely distributed and durable, they were available in either 110 or 220 volts. They were easily repaired and became an essential tool in gas stations and garages, and were, therefore, kept in good working condition for decades. Most of them, however, lived a hard life and are usually found in various stages of disrepair. Today, finding one in fine condition is very rare. This great piece isn't too hard to find in Europe in average condition, but its weight of nearly 30 pounds makes it too costly and impractical to ship anywhere. Side view: Luchard model *Collection Gilles Dutto*. Front view: Worthington model. France, 34 1/2" x 20 x 12 1/2". Rarity 8. $1,200

Small compressors, 1928. Made by R. Toussaint, France, this is one of the most popular Michelin objects among a very diverse group of collectors; it is easily obtainable in poor to average condition. The gauge housing, made of very brittle zinc like metal alloy called Zamac, is usually damaged or missing. However common it may be in rough shape, it has become very scarce in fine condition. It was available in four different voltages, 55, 110, 150 and 220 volts (usually stamped on the very front tip of the compressor). Round gauge version: 11 1/2" x 10 1/2". Rarity 8. $ 750; Square gauge version: 12" x 10" x 6 1/2". Rarity 9. $ 850 (Value based on a compressor in excellent original condition).

Latex figure, 1930s-1940s. Found in three sizes and materials (small 16" latex, medium 24" plaster, and large 32" papier maché) these usually were placed on the tops of salesmen service cars and delivery trucks, but weren't just limited to this use. One interesting detail only found in this particular Bibendum that really differentiates him from others, is his sash, which is tied with a bow on its side instead of being a continuous band. Beware of the reproduction of the small model, also made of latex but with a black painted underside and empty space between the feet. France, Rarity 10

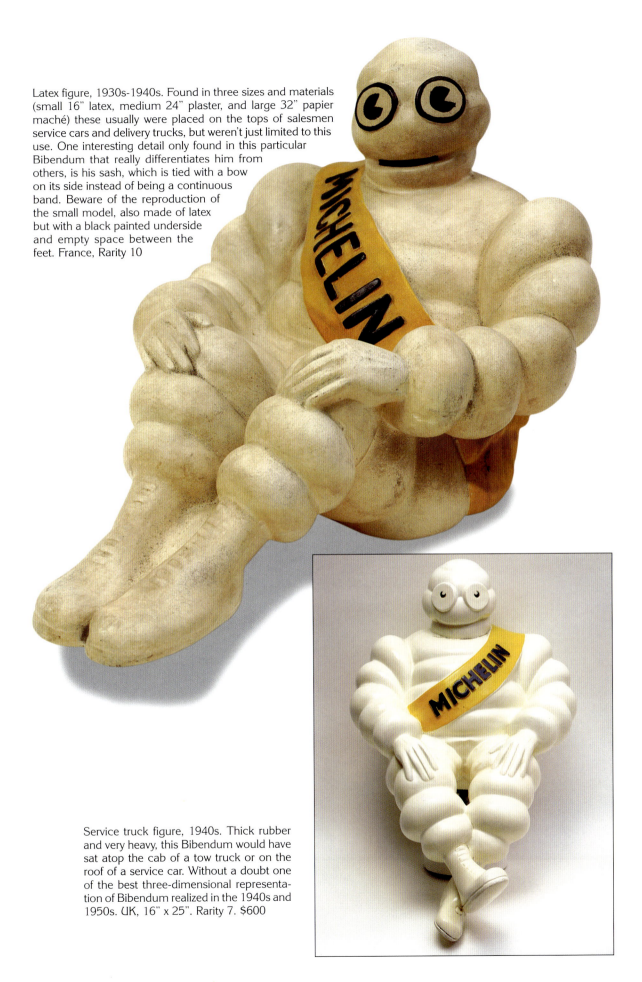

Service truck figure, 1940s. Thick rubber and very heavy, this Bibendum would have sat atop the cab of a tow truck or on the roof of a service car. Without a doubt one of the best three-dimensional representation of Bibendum realized in the 1940s and 1950s. UK, 16" x 25". Rarity 7. $600

Service truck figure, c. 1950s. Due to his square, sturdy base this Bibendum most often was used as a store display. France, 16 1/2" x 11". Rarity 8. $500

Service truck figure, c. 1950s to 1966. France 13" x 12". Rarity 7. $200

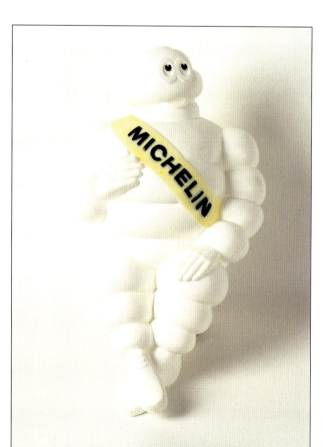

Truck figure, 1966 to present. Older models wired to be lit-up are especially desirable. This comes in two sizes, an 8 1/2" size often found mounted on trucks side view mirrors and an 18 1/2" size for mounting on top of truck cabins. *Collection Robert J Harrington.* New. $30; Older. $125.

Book store figure, 1960. Found where maps and guides would have been sold, this figure is one of the most sought after, especially the lamp version (factory wired). France 13" x 12" x 8 1/2". Rarity 8. $500

Thermoformed plastic light-up display, 1952, made by Lumineux R.B.C Paris. A very scarce piece due partly to its fragility. France 18" x 11 1/2". Rarity 9. $750

Garage light-up sign, 1960. Made by Hemmen & Jacquemin, this great three-dimensional light-up was used outdoors, mounted on service station walls like a flange sign. The smallest version of two is shown here. The Bibendum is removable and can be displayed on its own. France, 34" x 23". Rarity 8

Rubber figure, 1960s. Made of thick heavy rubber, this Bibendum is getting hard to come by. More likely a giveaway than a store display. USA, 13 1/2" x 8 1/2". Rarity 7. $125

Plastic figure, 1981. Very easily obtainable, but beware of plaster reproductions and some questionable ceramic versions. France, 12" x 8". Rarity 4. $30

Brochure holder, 1960s. A partitioned container made to look like a portion of tire is held up high by this huge Bibendum. With the topper generally missing, it is often thought to have been a tire holder. Finding this display complete and in nice condition is now rare. USA and Canada, 54" x 24. Rarity 8. $700

The headpiece of a Bibendum suit, c. 1940s, is an amazing object on its own. Older suits are incredibly scarce and, needless to say, very desirable. As far back as the early 1900s Michelin dressed up men in Bibendum suits to make the company's presence most noticeable and memorable. From automobile shows to carnivals, fairs and parades the Bibendums were there and not surprisingly still are today. Rarity 10

Complete Bibendum suit, c. 1960. These suits are practically impossible to obtain. A complete, suit in perfect condition, like this example, is a very rare sight. *Collection Martin Burger*. Life size. Rarity 9

Car mascot signed C. Paccagnini, Milan, c. 1907. A stunning piece, in my opinion, created to celebrate a huge victory for Michelin, when at the second "Targa Florio" race in Sicily in 1907. The first 9 cars to cross the finish line, lead by Felice Nazzaro in his Fiat, were all riding on Michelin tires and wheels. Michelin had just opened their factory in Turin, Italy, in 1906 and the publicity benefits from the victorious international race would certainly have been grand. To my knowledge this is the only known example. Italy, 4 3/4" tall. *Courtesy Finesse Fine Art*. Rarity 10

Car mascot, 1909. This elusive, primitive-looking Bibendum was offered in the 1909 Auto-Omnia catalog, as was the optional radiator cap shown here. The base is marked "Bibendum protége les pneus." Its rarity is such that, for years, it has lead collectors to argue over its existence as drawn in the Auto-Omnia catalog. It was also offered with a propeller for an additional 50 cents. Perhaps we can still argue about that one until it turns up. France, 4" tall. Hollow Metalo-bronze. *Collection Damian J Cessario.* Rarity 9

Car mascot, c. 1920. The stance, influenced by kick-boxing, is evident in this very scarce Bibendum. The sport of kick-boxing was made popular in France in the 1920s by Georges Carpentier who might have been the inspiration for this mascot. He became a national hero in 1920 as the world light-heavyweight champion. Silver-plated, hollow Metalo-bronze (Beware of solid bronze reproductions often plated). France, 3 7/8" tall. Rarity 9

Car mascot made by Generes & Cie, France, c. 1920, often referred to as "kneeling Bibendum" or "Bibendum scrutant l'horizon." Of all these amazingly rare Michelin mascots this one is the most attractive. Done on a slightly larger scale than the others, it is beautifully detailed down to inscriptions on the tire "Michelin Cablé" and the cufflinks on his wrists. Hollow silver-plated Metalo-bronze. (Beware of solid bronze reproductions often plated) Two examples shown, one on a nickel-plated radiator cap (*Collection Gilles Dutto*); and an incredible example with its plating intact mounted on a display base (*Collection Damian J Cessario*). France, 4 1/2". Rarity 9

Silver-plated trophy with three Bibendums holding up a cup. This amazing race trophy was probably made during the 1960s and kept in circulation for years as many trophies are. Another known version has a tall fluted vase instead of a cup. Spain, 6 7/8" x 5 1/2". Rarity 10

Trophy, c. 1980s. France, 7" tall. *Collection Martin Burger.* Rarity 7. $175

Trophy, 1990s. France, 5 3/8" without base. Rarity 6. $100

Trophies, c. 1960s. Some trophies were adapted as hood ornaments for Michelin's parade vehicles. It remains an object that can be found at a reasonable price, but not for long, as they are quickly finding their places in collections and becoming rather scarce. France, 5 1/8" x 2 3/4". Rarity 8. $350

Incredibly rare celluloid three-dimensional piece, c. 1920. The tire is marked "Câblé," which came on the market in 1919. It may have been mounted on a base. It may possibly have been a penholder for a desk, as the piece was designed to be attractive from all angles. It only stands 2 1/2" tall but it stands tall in Etienne Levillain's collection. Rarity 10

1929 original box to a Bibendum squeak toy, not the one shown here but a white example with the squeaker on its back. France, 4 3/4" x 6 7/8" x 3". Rarity 9

Solid rubber figures, 1930s. The aged rubber generally has a beautiful patina and some fine surface crackling. It has hardened, loosing all elasticity in the process. Beware of 1930s rubber items that lack these properties, they are likely to be more recent. France, 7" x 4 1/2". Rarity 8. $150

Hollow rubber figure, c. 1920. A very difficult figure to come by in nice condition because the aging rubber usually collapses in on itself, leaving the Bib with a deflated look. Very fragile and easily crushed, the aged rubber always hardens and is prone to cracking. Finding a decent condition example can be frustrating. France, 6" x 4 3/4". Rarity 9. $250

Solid rubber figure. This very nice piece was produced recently from a 1929 mould. It still makes for a very nice addition to one's collection. France, 6" x 4 1/4". Rarity 4. $50

Hollow rubber figure, 1950. France, 2 3/8" x 1 5/8". Rarity 8. $50

Squeak toy, 1950. This is a great figure that Michelin reproduced in the 1990s. The original one has become very affordable and easily obtainable, the reproduction is entirely white. France, 6 5/8" x 4 1/2". Rarity 5. $75

Thin hollow plastic figure, 1960s. A very unusual design, and a rarely seen figure. Holland, 4 1/4" x 3". Rarity 9. $125

Foam figure, 1950s. France, 3 1/2" x 4" wide. Rarity 7. $100

Figural plastic bank, c. 1950. This great bank is very scarce, due to the fragility of its early plastic. It is very rare to find one in decent condition. There is no maker's name on the truck itself, but the wheels are marked "Tootsietoy." I looked for this piece for years; it was well worth the wait. USA, 6" x 6". Rarity 9

From the early 1950s to today, small toys, key chains and gadgets have been produced in the likeness of Bibendum. They are too numerous for all to be photographed, but here are a few examples. The green Bib puzzle is scarce, it measures 3 1/4" high and is usually found in white and only 2" tall. The blue Bib 1970s flashlight is also an unusual item. The yellow tape measure (bottom right) was reproduced in recent years by Michelin.

Figural penholder, c. 1970. A nice, quality piece in heavy plastic with a metal base. France, 6 1/2" tall. Rarity 6. $150

Coin bank, 1950s to the present. Offered by Michelin to children of employees, blue for boys, pink for girls. UK. *Collection Martin Burger*. Rarity 7. $100

Figural AM radio, c. 1970. France, 7 1/2" x 4 1/2". Rarity 7. $175. The 1980s version has AM/FM with an antenna and a larger base, France. Rarity 6. $125

Chapter Seven
Paper Items

A collector is often a part-time detective when it comes to finding out information about something in his or her collection. The paper collectibles play a very important role in determining the age and origin of a sign or object. Whether it is a brochure or a magazine ad, it is likely to have been printed with a date. Paper items often hold the answers to many questions. Matching slogans found on letterheads, for instance, to a tin sign will prove to be quite accurate in determining the age. Other items, like, for example, the Bibendum magazines, feature many photographs showing advertising displays and gas stations around the world covered with Michelin signs. Some caution should be exercised, however. When looking at a vintage photograph, it is important to remember that signs were on buildings for many years. A sign may have been hung on a service station wall in 1910 and photographed in 1930. In short, the information contained in a photograph may be misleading if not correctly interpreted.

Very scarce articulated cardboard Bibendum, c. 1914. When the string is pulled, the arms and legs move up and down. USA, 10" x 11". Rarity 9. $750

Acrobat, 1926. Made of thick card stock printed on both sides, all pieces are riveted together. It was handed out to children at an automobile show in France in 1926. Printed by Bouquet, Paris 4 3/4" tall. Rarity 9. $350

Acrobat, 1928. Also of thick card stock, this version is printed with Bibendum only on one side. The other side gives instructions for cutting it out of a sheet and putting it together. France, 4 3/4" tall. Rarity 9. $200

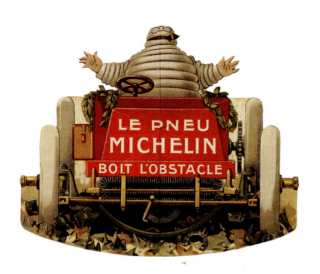 

Die-cut trade card, c. 1905. This very scarce, double-sided, foldout card, celebrating the Gordon-Bennett victory, is one of the earliest Bibendum images. France, 6" x 7 1/8". Rarity 9. $350

Artist rendering, c. 1908. This presentation board shows variations and options in tile installation and color scheme. Marked "Faienceries de Sarreguemines, Digoin Vitry Le François." France, 18" x 24". *Collection Robert J Harrington. Rarity* 10

1914 calendar on heavy card stock. Note the advertisement for the paper lantern on the top, the lantern would have been mailed out in the same envelope but to my knowledge none have ever resurfaced. The back of the calendar is printed with products available that year. France, 10 7/8" x 4 1/8". Rarity 9. $150

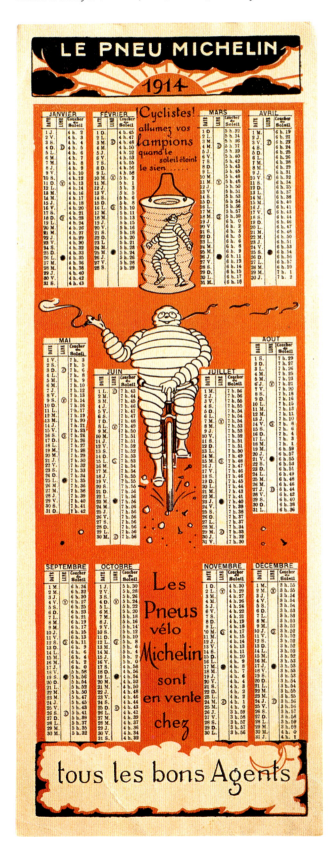

Poster stamps, c. 1910. The signs of the Zodiac, 12 in the series. Germany, complete set. Rarity 8. $175, individual stamps. Rarity 7. $10

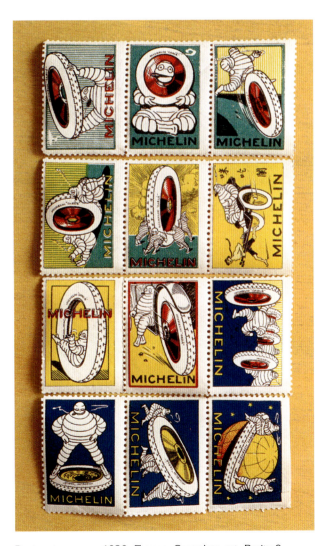

Poster stamps, c. 1920. France. Complete set, Rarity 9, $250; individual stamps, Rarity 8, $15

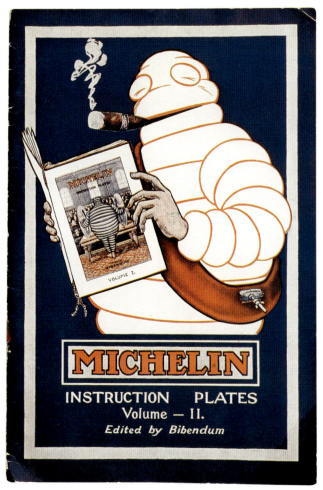

Tire users handbooks, 1914, 1915 and 1916. The great artwork was created specifically for the cover of these brochures. These are very desirable, with between 20 to 50 pages, depending on year, of great illustrations showing instruction plates on the do's and don'ts of using Michelin tires. USA, 10 1/2" x 7". *1914 brochure Collection Martin Burger.* Rarity 9. $150

"Théatre Illustré du pneu," 1912. Each manual is a compilation of approximately 24 ads from 1911 designed to function as a tire user's guide. France, 8 1/2" x 11 1/2". Rarity 7. $100

Bibendum magazine, 1923. Italy, 8 3/4" x 5 3/4". *Collection Peggy and Ed Strauss*. Rarity 8. $45

Bibendum magazine, 1932. Italy, 10 1/2" x 7 3/4". Rarity 8. $45

Bibendum magazine, 1933. Italy, 10 1/2" x 7 3/4". Rarity 8. $45

Bibendum revues, 1920s. These are full of great photos of dealerships, parades, showrooms, and some unique displays, along with, of course, many Bibendum suits from around the world. France. 9 1/2" x 6". Rarity 8. $40

Article from "Southern Automotive Dealer," 1929. Articles and photos like these are sometimes found in automobile related magazines. This one is about an advertising stunt. A Michelin tire was dropped 2000 feet out of an airplane, an event that drew a huge crowd.

 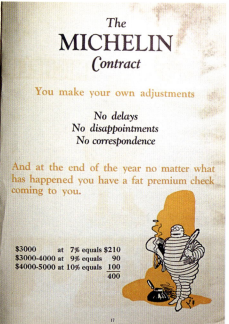

Salesman's aid, 1926. This very rare and very large book shows the possible profits for dealers and the advertising signs and displays available that year. USA, 14" x 20" *Collection Martin Burger.* Rarity 10

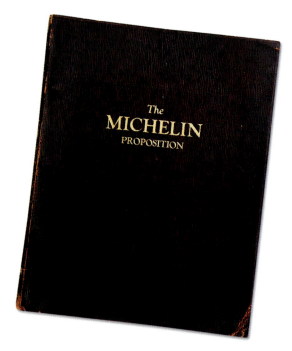

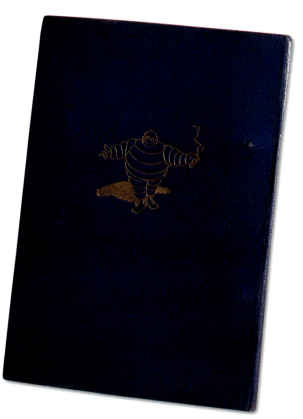

Documentation binder, 1928. Nicely embossed front and back cover, and full of useful information on accessories, tools, and signs. More than three quarters of the contents, however, are generally technical data sheets about tires. Michelin would routinely mail out new pages to keep the binders updated. France, 5 1/4" x 7 1/2" closed. Rarity 8. $75

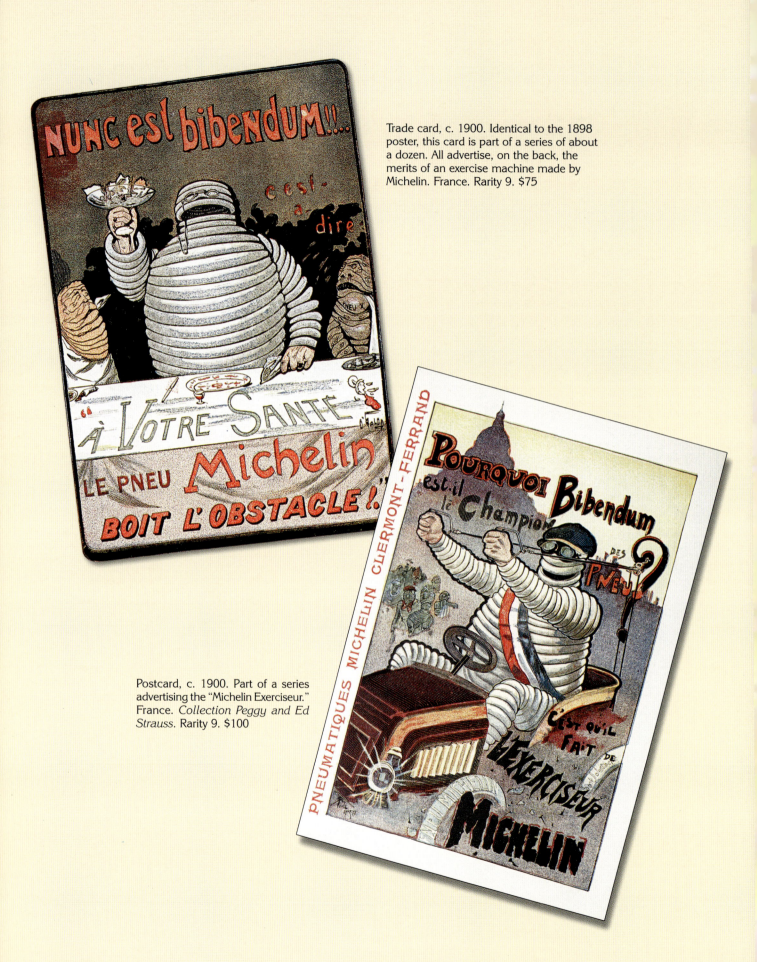

Trade card, c. 1900. Identical to the 1898 poster, this card is part of a series of about a dozen. All advertise, on the back, the merits of an exercise machine made by Michelin. France. Rarity 9. $75

Postcard, c. 1900. Part of a series advertising the "Michelin Exerciseur." France. *Collection Peggy and Ed Strauss.* Rarity 9. $100

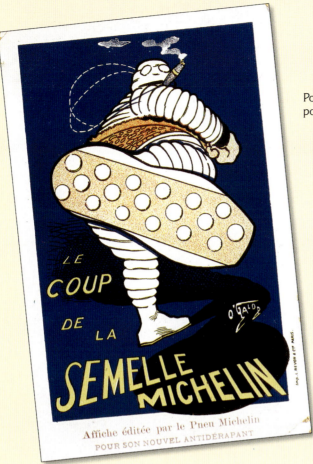

Postcard, 1905. Identical to the poster. France. Rarity 9. $75

Postcard, c. 1910. Holland. *Collection Peggy and Ed Strauss*. Rarity 9. $60

Postcard, 1910. Real photograph of man in an early suit on roller skates, these cabinet photos where often used as an illustrator's aid, putting men in situations and positions helped to give Bibendum more realistic and natural poses. UK 5 1/2" x 3 1/2". Rarity 9. $100

Postcard, c. 1910. "Carnaval de Nice." France. Rarity 6. $35

Postcard, c. 1910. "Carnaval de Nice." France. Rarity 6. $35

Postcard, 1915. "Carnaval de Nice." France, *Collection Peggy and Ed Strauss.* Rarity 9. $50

Postcards, c. 1910. Italy. *Collection Peggy and Ed Strauss*. Rarity 9. $125 each

Postcard depicting the 7th "Targa Florio" International race in Italy, 1913. Rarity 9. $150

Postcard, 1913. Italy. *Collection Peggy and Ed Strauss*. Rarity 9. $125

Postcard, c. 1915, advertising the poster by René Vincent, a 21" x 29" version of this very rare poster offered here for 10 cents. USA. Rarity 6. $35

Postcard, c. 1915. Souvenir of Steeplechase Park in Coney Island, New York, where the Michelin twins were a permanent attraction. USA. Rarity 9. $50

Postcard, c. 1915. Souvenir of "Portland Rose Parade Festival." USA. Rarity 9. $50

Postcard, c. 1915. The Michelin Twins win 1st prize in the New York City Automobile Carnival, USA. *Collection Brian E. Harto. Rarity* 9. $50

Micheline postcard, c. 1930. France. Rarity 7. $35

Micheline postcard, 1932. UK. Rarity 7. $35

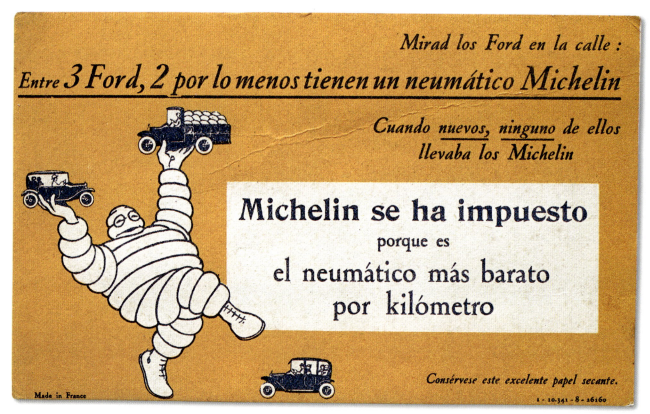

Ink blotter with Ford cars, 1926. This postcard is found in several languages, printed in France for export. 7" x 4 1/4". Rarity 8. $50

Blotter, 1928. France 7" x 4 1/2". Rarity 9. $50

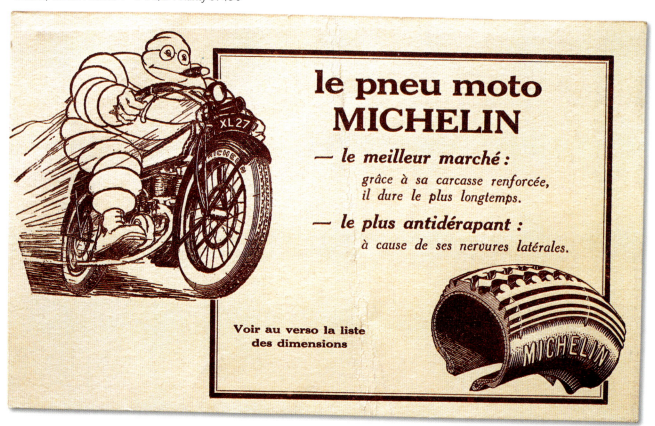

1920 Bookmark. Thick card stock, reverse side advertises "Cablé" tires. France 7 3/4" x 2 3/4". Rarity 9. $40

Bookmarks, c. 1920. Heavy card stock. USA, 2 1/2" x 6 3/4" *Collection Brian E. Harto.* Rarity 6. $25

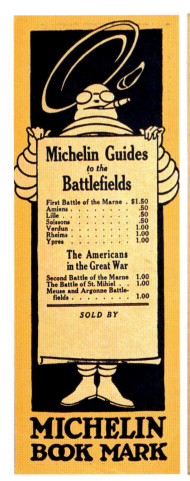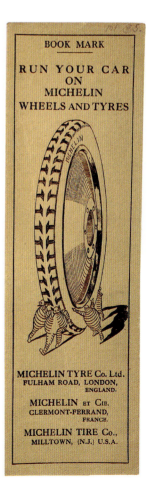

Instruction booklet for repairing tires and tubes, c. 1914. USA, *Collection Brian E. Harto.* Rarity 9. $35

Souvenir program of the Michelin Athletic Association, 1914. The formal opening of the Michelin field, donated to the town of Milltown. USA, 5" x 8". *Collection Brian E. Harto.* Rarity 10

Mailer, 1910. USA, approximately 8 1/2" x 11" opened. *Collection Brian E. Harto.* Rarity 10. $45

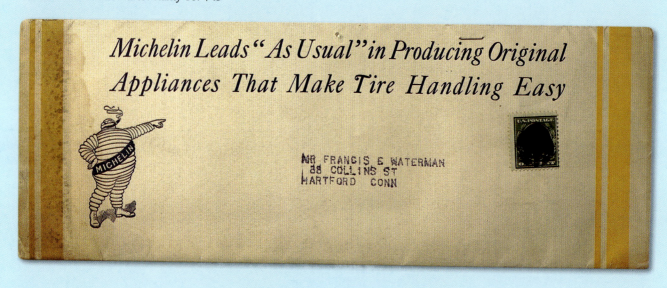

Directory of dealers in the USA, 1914. It is designed with a 3-D effect to look like a thick book, when in fact it is thin with only 62 pages. USA, 4 1/4" x 6 5/8" x 1/8" thick. Rarity 9. $75

Mailing card for accessories catalog, 1914. France, 5 1/12" x 3 1/2". Rarity 8. $15

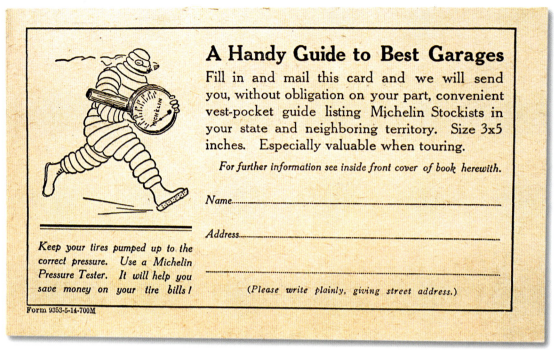

Mailing card to order a Michelin Stockist booklet by region, 1914. USA, 5 1/2" x 3 1/4". Rarity 9. $20

Mailing card to order an instruction book, 1914. USA, 5 1/2" x 3 1/14". *Collection Brian E. Harto.* Rarity 9. $20

1915 mailer. Heavy card stock, with illustrations by O'Galop. USA, 9 1/2" x 15". Rarity 9. $35

Trade card, 1915. Very scarce double-sided card. USA, 4 1/4" x 3 7/8". Rarity 9. $75

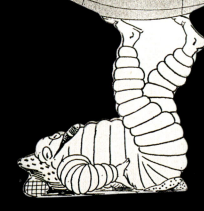

Trade card, 1914. As rare as its counterpart, this one is also double-sided. USA, 5 1/2" x 3 7/8". Rarity 9. $75

Price list for tires and accessories, 1921. USA, 6 1/4" x 3 1/4". Rarity 6. $10

Envelope, mid- to late 1920s. USA, 6 1/2" x 3 1/2". Rarity 8. $10

Letterhead, mid- to late 1920s. USA, 8 1/2" x 5 1/2". Rarity 8. $10

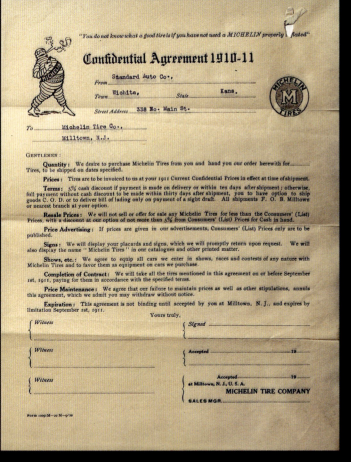

Contract, 1911. Confidentiality agreement between Michelin and a new dealer. USA. *Collection Brian E. Harto.* Rarity 9. $25

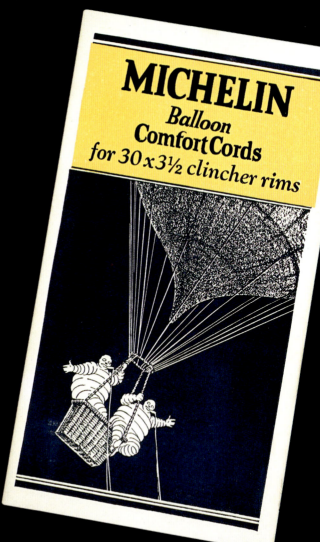

Brochure, 1924. USA, 6" x 3 3/8". Rarity 7. $15

Blank check with great graphics, c. 1915. Milltown, New Jersey, USA, 3 3/4" x 10 1/2". *Courtesy Milltown Museum, Milltown Historical Society.* Rarity 9

Inflation chart that accompanied a very rare compressed air bottle, c. 1920. France, 13 1/2" x 8 1/4". Rarity 10. $75

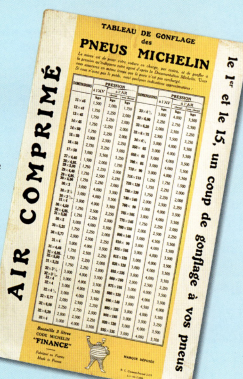

Die-cut pamphlet, c. 1910. France, 17 1/4" x 6 3/4". Rarity 10. $125

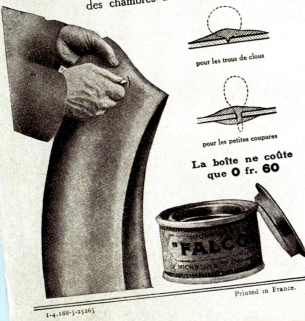

Flyer advertising mastic, code "Falcon," 1922. France, 5 1/2" x 4 1/4". Rarity 8. $20

Flyer advertising tire removing tools, 1923. Great graphics. France, 10 1/2" x 8 1/2". Rarity 8. $40

Brochure for the tire "Cablé-Comfort," 1923. France, 6 1/2" x 8 1/2" closed, 19" x 8 1/2". Rarity 8. $40

Brochure for the large compressor, 1928. France, 8 1/14"x 5 1/4". Rarity 9. $100

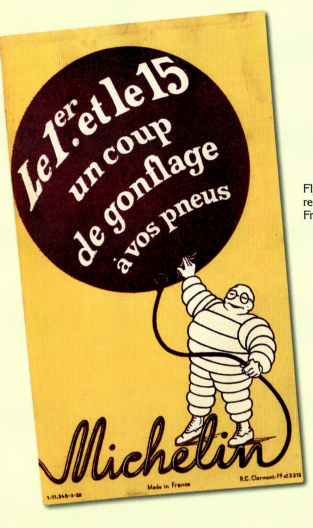

Flyer identical to the poster, 1928. It is a reminder to re-inflate your tires on the 1st and 15th of the month. France, 6 3/8" x 3 3/4". Rarity 8. $25

Flyer for Michelin toys, 1933. France, 10 1/2 x 8. Rarity 9. $75

151

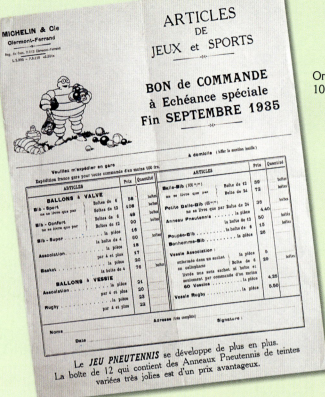

Order form for toys and game, 1935. France, 10 3/4" x 8 1/2". Rarity 5. $10

Magazine Advertisements

USA, 1910. $10-$15

USA, 1917. $10-$15

USA, 1918. $10-15

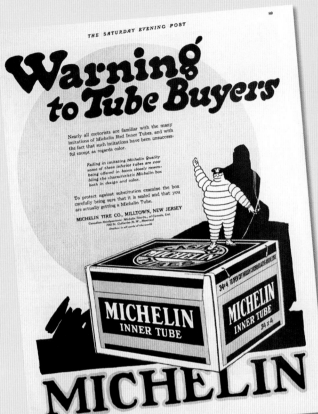

USA, 1919. $10-$15

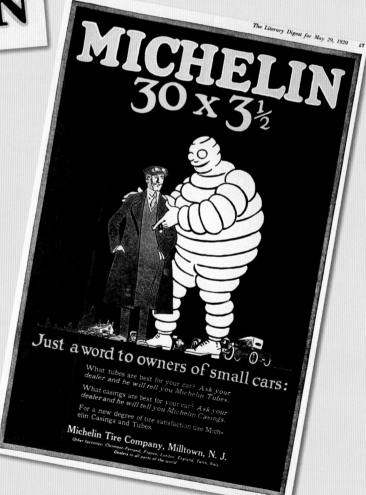

USA, 1920. $10-$15

USA, 1920. $10-$15

USA, 1920. $10-$15

USA, 1920. $10-$15

USA, 1920. $10-$15

USA, 1920. $10-$15

USA, 1920. $10-$15

USA, 1920. $10-$15

USA, 1922. $10-$15

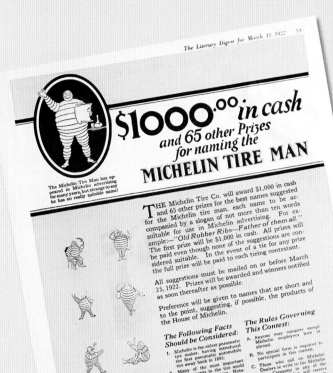

USA, 1922. $10-$15

USA, 1924. $10-$15

USA, 1926. $10-$15

France, 1913. $10-$15

France, 1914. $15-$20

"Auto Omnia" magazine ad, c. 1920. Very rare illustration by "Grand Aigle." France, 12 3/4" x 9". Rarity 9. $75

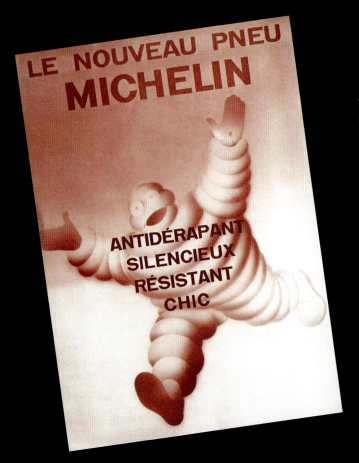

"L'illustration," large magazine ad, 1934. Very thick paper, often sold as a small poster because of its superior quality. France, Rarity 7. $ 75

Maps & Guides

First series of maps printed between 1910 and 1914. France. Rarity 7. $5-15

Back of a 1910 map.

1920s map. This series has the most colorful and interesting back covers. France. Rarity 7. $5-15

Back cover illustrations from the 1920s maps

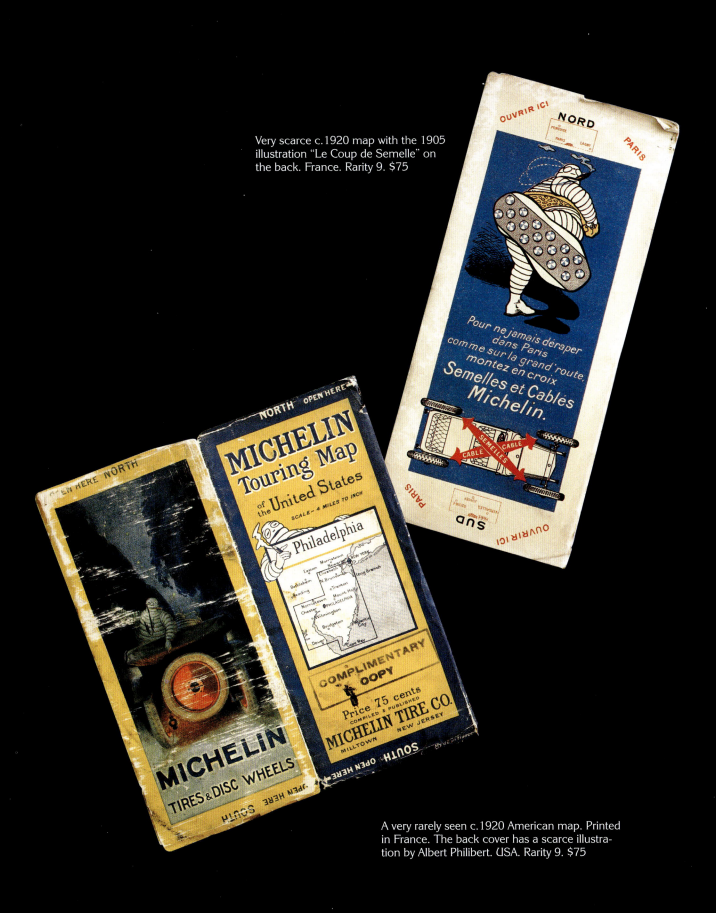

Very scarce c.1920 map with the 1905 illustration "Le Coup de Semelle" on the back. France. Rarity 9. $75

A very rarely seen c.1920 American map. Printed in France. The back cover has a scarce illustration by Albert Philibert. USA. Rarity 9. $75

Late 1920s to mid 1930s maps, France. Rarity 5-6. $5-15

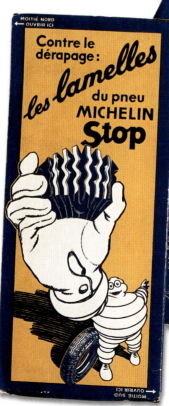

Late 1920s to mid 1930s maps back covers.

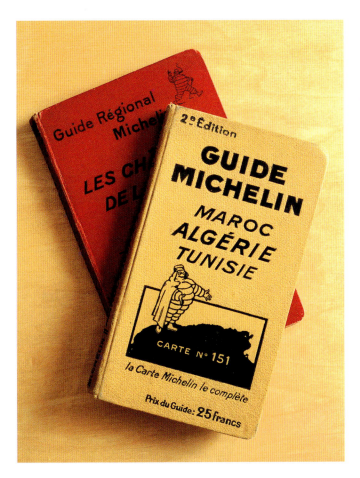

Michelin guides have been issued since 1900. Their value varies greatly depending on their age and condition. The first 10 years are generally the most sought after, though the 1939 American guide is at the top of the collector's list.

The 1939 American guide to France may be the most sought after guide, along with the elusive 1900 first edition. Printed by the Department of Defense in Washington D.C. It was the guide carried by US Officers during the landing in Normandy in June 1944. USA. Rarity 9

Chapter Eight
The Ultimate Tribute

This famous landmark in the London's Chelsea district first opened its doors in 1911. It was designed in 1909 by François Espinasse (1880-1925) under the strict supervision of the Michelin brothers, who had both graduated from "L'École des Beaux Arts," André as an architect and Édouard as a painter. Looking more like a monument to Bibendum than the Michelin headquarters in London, the structure had no equal. Even the Michelin building in Paris, which was also designed by Espinasse and was built in 1908 on Boulevard Péreire, was plain by comparison. The only similarities were the huge images of Bibendum on the façade (ceramic panels in Paris and stained glass windows in London) and a set of tiles depicting early car races, which was reproduced for the London building. Neither Edwardian nor Art Nouveau, the building had a style of its own. It could be perceived as being out of the imagination of someone who had no preconceived idea of what a building was supposed to look like, who had never seen one of any sort but only read about them in books. The use of such colorful tiles and gigantic stained glass windows was daring but necessary. After all what better place to build such a monument than its biggest competitor's (Dunlop) home land. The colossal structure was designed to serve many purposes. In addition to housing Michelin corporate headquarter offices it served as a depot, a showroom, and a tourism office, where a customer could have a complete itinerary drawn by a Michelin employee, while his newly purchased tires where fitted on his car. Practicality was key. The building was a tremendous success for Michelin.

In 1985, after nearly 75 years, Michelin decided to sell the building. It had not been used to its full potential for many years. Located in a prominent district in London, once on the market it received much attention from many developers. Fortunately for all Bibendum enthusiasts, Sir Terence Conran and his friend, Paul Hamlyn, became the new proprietors. They were able to tip the scale in their favor when they revealed to Michelin their intentions of refurbishing the building, giving it a new life as a bar and restaurant (Bibendum), a retail store (Conran Habitat), a publishing house (Hamlyn's business) and a multitude of new office spaces, all while keeping the original design of the Michelin façade.

No time was lost in starting the renovations, tiled walls were uncovered revealing lost treasures and many of the ceramic tiles were repaired or replaced as needed. Over 30 tiled images designed by Ernest Montaut famous for his early motoring racing scenes were restored. They depict the first place champions in their cars, equipped with Michelin tires, of course. The scenes of early races cover the length of the building and can also be found in the entrance hall. The Nunc Est Bibendum image is replicated in mosaic in a grand scale, on the floor of the building's main entrance, in addition to being found on the front façade as one of three stained glass windows. Another image of Bibendum riding a bicycle is on one side of the building and a representation of "Le coup de Semelle" is on the other. The wrought iron work throughout the building is exquisite, and original Michelin posters are on permanent display. No images or descriptions can come close to experiencing for yourself the pleasure of walking through those doors or seeing the building at night. Whether or not you collect Bibendum and early Automobilia, having a lunch or dinner in the Bibendum restaurant is an experience that you owe to yourself, and possibly the best way to thank Sir Terence Conran and Paul Hamlyn.

Stained glass window, front of the Michelin House. *Courtesy Bibendum Restaurant Limited.*

The Michelin House in London at night. *Courtesy Bibendum Restaurant Limited.*

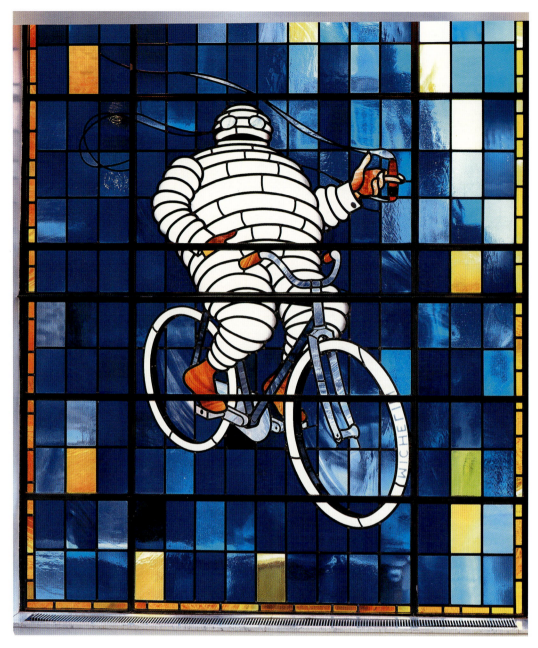

Stained glass window, side of the building. *Courtesy Bibendum Restaurant Limited.*

Stained glass window, side of the building. *Courtesy Bibendum Restaurant Limited.*

Chapter Nine
The Archives

Michelin manufactured tires in Milltown, New Jersey, from 1907 to 1930. Conventions in Milltown were a yearly occurrence. Assembling the top salesmen from across the country, they usually generated a wide array of awards, prizes and souvenirs, which are much sought after today by collectors. *Courtesy Milltown Museum, Milltown Historical Society.*

Delivery truck at the Milltown plant in the 1920s. *Courtesy Milltown Museum, Milltown Historical Society.*

Balloon launching at Baier's field in 1926. *Courtesy Milltown Museum, Milltown Historical Society.*

1920s Michelin marching band. Note Bibendum as the bandleader on the drum. *Courtesy Milltown Museum, Milltown Historical Society.*

The 1922 Milltown Michelin semi-professional baseball team had its own ball field, complements of Michelin. *Courtesy Milltown Museum, Milltown Historical Society.*

Original 1910 photograph. The back is marked "July 24th 1910, 3 pm, Marie and the Balloon Man." As strange as it is very rare, the only other known photo of this inflatable Bibendum is of Édouard Michelin holding it up in the air. It is very likely to be the first figural Bibendum made.

Interior photo of a tire dealer with a fantastic cardboard cutout sign of a Bibendum, c. 1913.

The vast majority of photos of the 1920s statues generally show them displayed outdoors, on lawns and sidewalks, or even mounted atop of pillars.

The great canvas banner on this truck is proof that so many Bibendum items still have to be discovered. *Courtesy Milltown Museum, Milltown Historical Society.*

Photos of men in Bibendum suits are always interesting especially early ones like this late 1920s example.

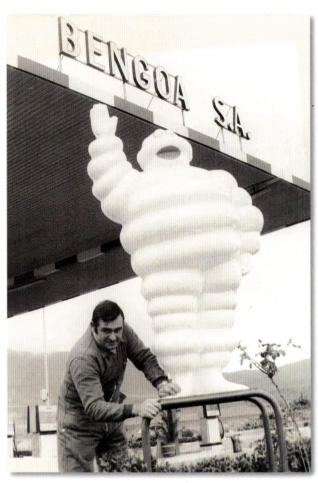

A very scarce 1960s three-dimensional light-up Bibendum at the entrance of a gas station in Spain. *Courtesy Patrimonio Histórico de Michelin España Portugal S.A. Reproducing this image in any form or by any means is prohibited without permission from Michelin España Portugal S.A.*

Service car with a great 1930s Bibendum atop the cab, used here as a demonstration vehicle for the "Super Comfort" tires, in front of a large crowd.

Our friend *Pau Medrano Bigas* assures us that garages decorated with Michelin tiles both interior and exterior can still be found in Spain, as proven in these recent photos.

Parting Words

I hope you enjoyed the book and feel that you have discovered a great deal of new information. I encourage you to contact me via regular mail and e-mail, especially if you have pre-1960s items in your collection that are not photographed or mentioned in this book. Whether it is to include in future editions or just to discuss a rare piece, I would be delighted to hear from you. I hope to be of assistance to collectors with items for sale or trade and collectors with particular wants, and of course I am always looking to add a rare piece to my own collection. But most of all, I look forward to sharing the passion of collecting advertising memorabilia.

Rudy Le Coadic
PMB 102
402 Graham Ave.
Brooklyn, NY 11211

rudymel@mindspring.com

Bibliography

Darmon, Olivier. *One Hundred Years of Michelin Man.* Paris, France: Editions Hoëbeke, 1997.

Dutto, Gilles. *Plus d'un siècle d'objets Michelin.* Châteauneuf, France: Gilles Dutto Editor, 2002.

Gonzalez, Pierre-Gabriel. *Bibendum, Publicité et objets Michelin.* Paris, France: Editions du Collectionneur, 1995.

Gonzalez, Pierre-Gabriel. *Bibendum à l'affiche. Cent ans d'Image Michelin.* Paris, France: Michelin & Cie, 1998.

Milltown Centennial Committee. *Images of America: Milltown.* Dover, New Hampshire: Arcadia Publishing, 1995.

Index

Ashtrays, 89-92
Banks, 114, 115
Baseball, 140, 172
Bookmarks, 139
Calendars, 73, 119
Car mascots and trophies, 107-111
Cardboard signs and displays, 12, 16-20, 173
Clocks, 72-76
Compressors, 18, 99, 100, 125, 150, 151
Desk set, 93
Flange signs, 24-26, 37, 46, 47
Glass slide, 81
Handbooks and manuals, 120, 121, 124, 125, 140, 141, 145, 147, 150
Hats, helmet, 94, 95
Ink blotters, 138
Key chains, 77, 81, 115
Lamp, 93
Lighters, 88
Light-up signs, 47, 76, 103, 104
Magazines and ads, 120-124, 153-162
Maps and guides, 162-167
Marble plaque, 93
Matchbooks, 87
Micheline, 95, 137
Mirrors, 31
Original photos, 171-174
Original renderings, 118
Paper figures, 116-118
Paper, miscellaneous brochures, letterheads, and envelopes, 56, 65, 66, 69, 70, 120-125, 138-152
Pennant, 94
Pins, brooch, buttons, medals and jewelry, 77-81
Playing cards, 83
Porcelain signs, 25, 26, 28, 32, 33, 36-42
Postcards, 126-137
Poster stamps, 119
Posters, 11-20
Pressure gauges, 61-69
Printing blocks, 82
Radio, 115
Sewing kit, 81
Suit, 106, 124, 128, 174
Thermometers, 46
Three-dimensional figures, 89-92, 96-115, 151, 172-174
Tiles, 45, 175
Tin signs and displays, 21-27, 29-31, 33-37, 41, 43-47, 68, 71
Tins and boxes 48-66, 68, 71, 73, 74, 112, 149
Tools 48, 49, 53, 56, 61-70, 99, 100, 125, 149
Toys 18, 19, 95, 96, 105, 112-115, 117, 151, 152
Trade cards 116, 118, 141-144
Wallets and other leather items 84-87, 67, 75
Wood and Masonite signs 27, 45-68, 71